SHE MADE ME LAUGH

Mother Teresa and the Call to Holiness

SHE MADE ME LAUGH

Mother Teresa and the Call to Holiness

STEPHANIE EMMONS

PARACLETE PRESS
Brewster, Massachusetts

2020 First Printing

She Made Me Laugh: Mother Teresa and the Call to Holiness

Copyright © 2020 by Stephanie Emmons

ISBN 978-1-64060-184-0

Library of Congress Cataloging-in-Publication Data
Names: Emmons, Stephanie, 1969- author.
Title: She made me laugh : Mother Teresa and the call to holiness / Stephanie Emmons.
Description: Brewster, Massachusetts : Paraclete Press, 2020. | Summary: "A memoir of direct experiences with Mother Teresa, when Emmons discovered her sense of humor first hand, and is also a reflection on the saint's "dark night of the soul""-- Provided by publisher.
Identifiers: LCCN 2020014722 | ISBN 9781640601840
Subjects: LCSH: Teresa, Mother, Saint, 1910-1997. | Emmons, Stephanie, 1969---Travel--India.
Classification: LCC BX4700.T397 E46 2020 | DDC 271/.97 [B]--dc23
LC record available at https://lccn.loc.gov/2020014722

10 9 8 7 6 5 4 3 2 1

Published by Paraclete Press
Brewster, Massachusetts
www.paracletepress.com

Printed in the United States of America

CONTENTS

	INTRODUCTION	9
1	SOMETHING BEAUTIFUL	13
2	THE TRIP OF A LIFETIME	16
3	MISERABLE IN THE CITY OF JOY	29
4	SO SARI	32
5	TRAINING	39
6	NO ROOM AT THE "Y"	45
7	UNCLE FRANK	54
8	CULTURE SHOCK	61
9	FINDING MOTHER TERESA	64
10	THE BODY OF CHRIST	72
11	THE HOLY FAMILY	81
12	RUNNING ON EMPTIES	85
13	I'M JUST ONE PERSON	88
14	HAPPINESS IS A FRESH TURKEY SANDWICH	92
15	HAVING NOTHING, AND YET POSSESSING EVERYTHING	98
16	LEAVING MOTHER TERESA	101
17	A VALENTINE'S HOMECOMING	104
18	UNBELIEVABLE	109
19	IF THERE BE GOD	117
20	IT CHANGED EVERYTHING	125
21	SHE SUFFERS AND SHE LAUGHS	127
22	TWO HEARTS	132
23	A SAINT TO THE SKEPTICS	135
24	THE CALL TO HOLINESS OR, IF YOU WANT TO BE A SAINT	139
25	HE MADE THEM LAUGH	144
	AFTERWORD	147
	ACKNOWLEDGEMENTS	151
	NOTES	155

To

Catherine and Loi, the lights of my life. Thanks for your patience and understanding these past few years when I often had to divide my time, energy, and attention between you and the book. Thank you for helping me find joy in the present moment and for making it easy to laugh at myself.

And to

Miriam Browning . . . without you this whole adventure never would have happened! Thanks for making me laugh.

INTRODUCTION

I n January of 1996, when my friend Miriam and I were in our twenties, we followed our mutual dream and traveled to India. Our aim: to help the poor in Calcutta and, hopefully, to meet Mother Teresa.

We had wanted to see her community, the Missionaries of Charity, in action and hoped they would let us roll up our sleeves and jump in alongside them. So, once we got settled in Calcutta, found out Mother Teresa's address and mapped out our route, Miriam and I just walked over and showed up at her door.

As we had hoped, the sisters were gracious and happy to have us. They ushered us right in and we got to meet Mother Teresa that very day. And it was just that simple. I'm not sure what I had expected. But I do recall hoping that, if we did get to meet her, we might witness some really cool saintlike quality or manifestation—something. But she didn't levitate. No glowing halo crowned her head, no great throng of followers hung on her every word. There was nothing like that. And though she must have received thousands of visitors over the years, Mother Teresa was patient and welcoming to Miriam and me when we met her.

What has stayed with me all these years is the kindness in her eyes. But there was something I didn't expect: her sense of humor. She made me laugh. Not just once, but every time we met her. It seemed to come naturally—an easy kind of joking around. I remember thinking that aside from her being a living saint, I liked her as a person. She didn't seem self-conscious or shy. She was the kind of person who puts you at ease and makes you want to hang around, even if it was just to shoot the breeze. She was just there—simple, funny, intense. And perfectly ordinary.

This book shares some parts of the travel journal I began during the trip, letters I sent home, and reflections I've written in the years since. And while there are plenty of, "Wow! We're in India!" moments, I also talk about some of the darker parts of the trip for me. I had wanted to go to India since I first learned of Mother Teresa when I was a kid. But once I actually got there, things took a downward turn. I was overwhelmed by pretty much everything.

In the years following Mother Teresa's death in 1997, some of her private writings surfaced. They told a story of a woman in love with God, but a woman who also knew great spiritual pain. As I had naturally assumed that Mother Teresa's life was pretty much one of profound, unbroken closeness to God, I, like many others, was flabbergasted. I came across an article in *Time* magazine which did this big exposé. They titled it "Mother Teresa's Crisis of Faith," which effectively turned the world on its ear. One of the people they interviewed, Father

James Martin, SJ, echoed my own feelings when he asked, "Who would have thought that the person who was considered the most faithful woman in the world struggled like that with her faith?"

I've had a hard time coming to terms with all of this. Even more surprisingly, though, was the discovery that that playfulness and good humor I had seen, and the pain she described in her letters—these could be present at the same time. It wasn't necessarily one or the other. In fact, apparently, it's a very real aspect in the spiritual life, this both/and theme—one that mystics and saints have long been acquainted with. I came to learn that maybe there's much more to her story—and our story—than might be discernible at first blush.

But I'll start at the beginning, back in the peculiar days of pet rocks, bell bottoms, and peace symbols: 1979 . . .

1 SOMETHING BEAUTIFUL

The year was 1979. My grade six buddies and I, sporting our polyester seventies wear, were chatty and excited. It wasn't every day we got to watch a film at school. Our teacher had said that this one was called *Something Beautiful for God*. We were all sitting cross-legged on the orange shag carpet in the library at Pope John XXIII School in Ottawa, Canada. My friend Lisa and I sat with our knees touching; we were always together. Then someone turned out the lights and the show began.

I saw the image of a small woman with dark skin and a white outfit. "Who's that?" I asked, looking up at Mrs. McGetrick, the school librarian who was standing beside me. "Shh . . ." she said slowly with a little smile, a straight index finger pressed to her lips. Then in a whisper, "You'll see." What I saw on the screen over the next hour struck a strange chord in me. The music was sad, and the woman was slowly walking toward the camera, holding a scrawny child by the hand. Neither of them looked too cheerful. I didn't understand what was going on, but I was spellbound. There was something about her.

The narrator said that her name was Mother Teresa and that she was helping the poor and the sick. There were kids in the streets, people in beds, babies in cribs, and more ladies in white. When it was over, the lights came on and everyone started chatting noisily. I remember looking around to see if anyone else looked like they were about to cry. Mrs. McGetrick said that Mother Teresa must be a very special nun to have given her whole life to God and to helping the poor people.

The poor people? I wondered. *Why were they poor? How come they were living on the streets and in the train stations? Who were these kids, and why weren't their moms and dads looking after them?*

I can still clearly recall the look on Mother Teresa's face, and I could have sworn she was looking right at me. There was so much on her face. At times she looked warm and kind, but at other times, a little scary. She looked almost angry. I tried to make sense of this. But then, our teacher told us to line up and we headed back to class.

I couldn't stop thinking about it—the film, the children, and their sad faces. And her face. I couldn't stop thinking about Mother Teresa's face.

Soon after seeing that film, I had a dream I was in India talking with her. She smiled her kind smile at me, and I felt her warm presence. Then I was back at home, alone in my room, dreaming I was talking to God: "I want to meet her! I want to join them and help the poor people! But how will I ever get to India? How can I explain this to Mom and Dad? Will they even let me go?" God then replied, "You'll know when the time is right, but you have to wait."

Waiting is hard at any age, but it is especially so at 11 when you suddenly know exactly what you're meant to do. Frustrated, but undaunted, I continued, "God, why did you show me this and make me want to go there so badly if all I can do is wait? How long?" I demanded. Then, gently, "You're young and you're not ready. You'll have to wait, sweetheart." With all the grown-up conviction I could gather, I shot back, "I'm ready! I really am, Father." He spoke again, this time with a little more conviction: "Stephie. It's not time yet." And with that, I woke up.

It seemed so real.

I was exasperated. I simply could not imagine why He wouldn't just make it happen right then and there. I was good and ready and felt sure I would make a very good nun.

Sixteen years later, I stood in front of her for real, and her smile was just as kind and her presence just as warm as I had imagined. . . .

2 THE TRIP OF A LIFETIME

One sunny day in August of 1995, when I was 27, I was at my best friend Margie's apartment having coffee. We had both lost someone very special not long before: Margie, her mom, and me, my Grandma Emmons. We were both still getting over the shock, coffeeing our way through our grief together.

The phone rang. It was our mutual friend, Miriam Dowd. We had met Miriam about six years earlier through Challenge, a Catholic youth community we all belonged to in Ottawa. I could tell from Margie's side of the conversation that something was up. Margie had long known of my affinity for Mother Teresa and was smiling and nodding, stirring my curiosity.

"Hmmm. Hang on a moment, okay, Miriam?" Margie said.

Then, Margie turned to me. "Steph, Miriam is planning a six-week trip to India next January to work with Mother Teresa and she's looking for someone to go with her. Can you think of anyone?"

After pondering the question for about ten seconds, I said, "Yeah, okay!"

It was no more notable than if I had just accepted an invitation to go to the movies. And so, after a few weeks of pinching myself to make sure it was real and convincing my poor family that I had not lost my mind, we got busy making all of the preparations, getting the required shots and arranging the travel.

A few days before our departure, Miriam's brother, Father Thomas Dowd (now a bishop), celebrated a cozy send-off Mass at their parents' home for us. There, I took Father Tom aside and told him not to worry, that I would look after his little sister. He smiled and said, "Oh I have a feeling she'll be looking after you." How right he was.

When the big day arrived, January 7, 1996, I went to Mass by myself in the morning at St. Maurice Church. During the homily, our pastor told the congregation about our trip and pointed me out. He asked them to reach out and pray a blessing on me, and with that, every one of them extended a hand toward me, praying for my safety and wellbeing. My whole parish. I felt peaceful the rest of the day. Meeting up with Miriam and our family and friends who had come to wish us bon voyage, I set about the difficult business of saying goodbye to my mother and my brother Rob who had come to see me off. They were understandably concerned, reluctant to see me heading so far away toward the unknown. Ultimately though, they supported me and wanted me to do what made me happy.

At long last, we were in the air heading from Ottawa to Halifax. We giggled an awful lot during the first movie. It was *Babe*—the one with the talking pig and the dancing farmer.

Three little blind mice kept appearing, and the sight of them sent us both into peals of silent laughter. (You can only laugh so loud and so long on a plane before your fellow passengers start to get perturbed. . . .) We didn't dare make eye contact for fear of setting each other off again. We were both giddy and emotional, as the enormity of what we were doing started hitting home. Besides, the weeks leading up to this day had been busy and nerve-wracking, so this bit of comic relief was welcome.

Eventually, we each settled into our own solitude. I thought about the days and weeks ahead, trying to somehow prepare myself for what was to come. But how do you do that? This was India. I'm from Canada; there was no frame of reference. And other than Miriam, I wouldn't know a soul there. I was nervous, for sure. But more than that, I was thrilled. This was the trip of a lifetime! Every moment would be entirely new and different, and I was keen to get at it.

Before long, however, I started feeling very unwell, thinking maybe a migraine was coming on. There was sharp pain in both my ears, right down into my throat. I was almost in tears when we called for the flight attendant to ask for help. This must happen to other people, as they knew just what to do. They gave me two small white plastic cups with hot moist paper towels inside them to hold over my ears to relieve the pressure. I guess I had a bit of a cold and the change in pressure bothered my ears and sinuses. Miriam, though very sympathetic, couldn't help giggling at the sight of me. In her defense, I'm sure I did look silly, maybe like Yoda with round white plastic ears, but I didn't care. The warm towels really helped.

By the time we stopped in Halifax, I couldn't hear out of my right ear, but I was just glad the pain had eased. On the second descent, this time in Amsterdam, I had an even rougher time than the first. My ears hurt so much that I was crying. Once we landed at Schiphol Airport in Amsterdam, I bought some nose drops and used them several times during the next flight. I also bought some ibuprofen and made sure to take it before our descent. Thankfully I was okay. I just kept chewing gum, yawning, swallowing, and praying, and I was okay. It was a long, long day. But *so* worth it.

We arrived in Bombay Airport and were funneled into a large room where we lined up with a throng of others to show our passports and go through customs. The baggage retrieval area was crazy. A crush of travelers, luggage handlers, and people begging swallowed us up as we slowly made our way to the front. It took a good half hour to find our bags, and we then proceeded through an X-ray machine. Then we found our way to the Indian Airlines gate—one staff person with one phone sitting at a wooden desk. We asked about our flight to Cochin—the final aerial leg on our trip!—and he told us to go outside and walk through the parking lot to the bus marked Indian Airlines. It was 3:30 a.m. and very dark. As we walked out to the parking lot, cabbies approached us hollering "taxi!" at us over and over. It was unnerving. We reached the bus and climbed aboard. The driver, two men, and a young couple all stared at us as we stood there awkwardly at the front. The driver asked to see our plane tickets, gestured toward the seats and stowed our bags. All around us nothing stood still—old style taxis, zippy motorized rickshaws, noisy buses, and just so many cars. This was our first experience of the chaos. We took our seats and waited quietly in the rickety old bus for about twenty minutes.

Then we left for the other terminal where we would catch the flight to Cochin. I felt weird and a bit frightened. My stomach was in knots. Now it was 4 a.m., which is a sort of dark and scary time to begin with. We were so alone on a strange bus in a very strange city with a very bad smell. We passed numerous shacks by the side of the road in Bombay, most made with cardboard and rusty tin siding. People, we realized, were in those shacks—whole families—sleeping. Miriam and I glanced at each other, and then we just stared out the window in silence the rest of the way. That bus trip somehow made me sick—soul sick. It had begun.

Almost thirty hours had passed since Miriam and I had first left home. The endless hours spent sitting in airports, on tarmacs, and in the air had hardly given us a chance for any decent stretches of sleep. We were beat. Here's a letter I wrote to my best friend, Margie, while waiting in the Bombay airport:

Dear Margie,

Hello from two tired, jet lagged, fed up travelers! We are sitting in Bombay airport, waiting hours and hours for our next flight. The trip has been hard but we're almost there! Two flights down, one to go. Cochin, here we come! I can't wait to get on the next plane—hope I can sleep a bit. Schiphol Airport in Amsterdam was HUGE! I think it might be the biggest one in the world but I'm not sure. We actually got lost a few times in there, but it was ok cause our next flight was delayed three hours. The shops were so expensive and so was the food. I paid $9.50 for a bowl of tomato soup! Crazy compared to the $4 or so we'd pay in a restaurant at home. We found a lounge where travelers were all stretched out across chairs. It didn't look too comfy but it was better than nothing so we did the same. We were able to catch a couple of winks, despite the constant flight announcements, fluorescent lighting, zillions of people, and the SMOKE! Everyone smokes here. Ugh. On our overseas flight there were little monitors on the ceiling showing us where we were. We flew over or near: London, Brussels, Berlin, Paris, Munich, Rome, Barcelona, Frankfurt, Glasgow, Manchester, Hamburg, and more! So cool. Anyway, I've had about 3 hours of sleep in the past 27 and Miriam has had about 5. I'm so freakin tired and a bit delirious. We seem to be laughing a lot. Everything is hilarious when you're overtired. But we

are safe and really excited to get to Cochin and meet Father
John in a few hours. I'm thinking of all of you in the snow
back home as I swat away the mosquitos and move slowly
in the heavy humidity here in India. (India! It's hitting me
. . . I made it!) No complaints though—I love the heat. And
aside from eating dinner at breakfast time and vice versa,
we're holding up fairly well. Can't wait to tell you everything
in person.

Bye for now. I'll write again as soon as I can.
Love Steph

I finished the letter and we heard the long-awaited boarding
call for our flight, quickly gathered up our things and scrambled
to the tarmac toward the very last plane—the one that would
take us to Cochin. And although I was thrilled that we would
soon be there, I was desperate to close my eyes.

Once settled, I curved my little travel pillow around my
neck. And, pulling my fleece jacket up to my ears like a cozy
blanket, I relaxed and became one with the seat. At last I could
rest. Closing my eyes, I slipped out of consciousness. It was
delicious. Then a loud female voice jolted me awake. I thought
it had only been a few minutes but apparently an hour had
passed. It felt like a wicked hangover. I rubbed my eyes, feeling
fuzzy, disoriented, and annoyed. The voice was announcing that
we were almost there, and it was time to prepare for landing.

Miriam and I looked out the window, suddenly wide awake with the happy knowledge that we were about to land. We saw lots of water, waving palm trees, and a few buildings. Looking at each other with silly grins, Miriam whispered, "We're in India!" A few minutes later, we landed in Cochin in the south of India. I was so excited.

As I stepped off the plane, the heat embraced me like a warm, wet blanket. Back home in Canada, we had bundled up against January's biting cold. Now we were in the heat of a tropical country, and it was heavenly. Our big adventure was finally underway. Our hosts, Father John and three religious sisters, were there to meet us. Friends of Miriam's had traveled to India and stayed with them the previous year. These friends had put us in touch with Father when we started making plans months earlier. He was delighted to have us come.

The little welcoming committee came rushing toward us, all smiles and chatter and waving arms. They greeted us heartily, like long-lost friends, though we had never met. We would stay with them for the first two weeks.

Here's part of a letter I sent home once we arrived in Cochin and got settled:

Okay Margie, we made it!
We arrived in Cochin with no problems. Father and some nuns met us at the airport. Their driver, Baby,

carried our bags. The ride from the airport to the place where we were staying was crazy! You know Mr. Toad's Wild Ride at Disney World? It was like that. And picture this: one narrow road, no dividing line, driving on the left, many, many motorcycles, rickshaws, bicycles, Mack trucks, taxis, and people walking everywhere. It seems they communicate mostly by honking. I was startled many times, but it was thrilling! Miriam and I had to hold onto the seats in front of us for dear life. I kept closing my eyes. We couldn't stop laughing so hard, like when you're on a terrifying roller coaster, trying not to scream! Miriam's awesome. She makes me laugh a lot. We had a good long sleep last night and I'm feeling much better. This morning, we were offered three varieties of bananas. I tried some of each and they weren't too bad. I really wish I didn't hate bananas. Miriam loved them. And here is my great news of the century: On Feb 9, Mother Teresa is coming here to Cochin! MOTHER TERESA! It's the 100th anniversary of the Catholic Diocese here and she is coming to give the keynote address! Father has known about it but he waited to tell us in person. And get this—he said he would see if we could meet her! I can't believe this. By then, we will have been to Calcutta and back, and who knows—maybe we'll have met her there already. Wow. Oh, and this morning we washed our clothes in buckets, outside on the roof. The sisters showed us how to scrub them on a slab of rock. The view from up there was stunning. Well we're off to find a

bank so we can cash some travelers' checks. The sisters are
taking us shopping for saris! Loving this.
  Miss you.
  Love Steph

My first few days there were all about the senses. Everything
was so new and fresh. In many ways, it was good.

One morning, Father John took us to a little roadside fruit stand
and bought several pineapples. The man there said they had been
picked that morning. He cut one open with a massive, ancient
machete and offered a piece to each of us. The glowing yellow flesh
was sweeter and yummier than any candy I'd ever tasted, and I
know candy. In Canada we pay an awful lot for pineapples, despite
the fact that days or weeks pass between the picking and the
eating. But in India, these beauties cost the equivalent of pennies.
We went so crazy over them that Father bought a whole bunch for
us to take home. They didn't last beyond the day.

I went up on the roof alone whenever I had the chance. I
liked being around people and all, but I'm also an introvert, so
I grabbed moments of solitude when I could. I loved sitting up
there in my little sanctuary, looking out over the towering tops
of banana trees. I'd never been a fan of bananas before the trip
(okay . . . hated them) so I wasn't exactly swooning over them
as I had the pineapples. But they still beat the heck out of any
banana I'd ever tasted back in Canada.

When I called home and talked to my brother Rob, a few days after our arrival, I was endlessly complaining about the heat. It had sometimes hit 40 degrees Celsius (104 degrees Fahrenheit) and I don't do so well in the heat. He then said he had just come in from a half hour of shoveling after a huge snowfall. That shut me right up. I didn't miss the Canadian winter one bit, although it occurred to me several times every day that I was very far from home.

Numerous times over the next six weeks, whenever it occurred to us, Miriam and I would gleefully exclaim to one another, "We're in India!" It was fun to say and just such a bizarre thing to hear. Plus, it was so hard to believe that we were actually there, I think we were trying to make it sink in. Pretty sure it never really did.

Not everything was rosy, though. Here's part of another letter I sent home:

Dear Margie,

I want to tell you a bit more about my first day here in Cochin. It was a very hard one. We'd been traveling about thirty hours and I had only been able to sleep about three hours in total. So I was absolutely exhausted—as bone tired as I've ever been. We finally touched down in Cochin in the south of India, and a very friendly Father John was at the airport to meet us. I almost cried. I think I'd been secretly worried that no one would be there and we'd be left to fend for ourselves. But no, there he was, along with his driver named Baby. I felt the warmth of reassurance wash over me, like God was saying, See? I told you I'd look after you. After the introductions and getting settled in the car, we were treated to that jarring and jolting thrill of our first experience in traffic. Wow. It was nerve wracking but strangely fun too.

Then we arrived at the place where we'll stay for the first week—the residence of a priest and several nuns. We asked Father if we could use the phone to call home and he said we could. He showed us to his office and I called my Mom. She was thrilled to hear from me. We started catching up and she said she missed me a lot and had been wearing my scarf. I was so thrilled that I could finally tell her all about the trip, my worries, and whatever else I wanted. There was so much to say! Then for some reason, Father took the phone out of my hand and said, "Hi Mom! Don't worry, she's in good hands with Father, okay? Bye now!" and he hung up the phone. Just like that. She was gone. I felt like I'd been shot. I was so exhausted and I needed so much to talk to my Mom and was nowhere near finished. Of course I knew she would be very upset too. I burst into tears (mostly anger) and he grabbed my face and buried it in his chest, sort of petting my cheek over and over, saying, "There, there, no need to cry! Your Father is here. Why are you crying? You must miss your mother a lot." I was beside myself, crying hard as I pushed away from him. He looked bewildered, as if he truly had no idea why I was so upset. He told Miriam she could make her call. I said I was going to our room, bolted from the office and ran all the way.

When I reached my room, I jumped on my bed and just sobbed. I was thinking I could only phone when he said so, that he'd be around all the time, etc. I felt desperate to be back home. I was still bawling my head off when Miriam walked in. I unloaded my feelings, holding nothing back. She was supportive but seemed very worried. I told her I was going to set my boundaries and tell him off. I had to tell him where I stood! I was feeling pretty bold in my hurt, sleep-deprived state. Poor Miriam . . . I think she was really concerned. Here we were on the very first day and I was about to alienate our host—one of the few people we knew in the city . . . in the country! She asked me to have a good sleep before I said anything to him. I agreed. It turned out to be a very good idea because in the morning I did gain some perspective and didn't quite feel so raw or injured after I had slept. Thank God for Miriam who saved me from myself. At breakfast Father assured us that the next time we wanted to call someone all we had to do was ask, and we could talk as long as we liked. Gotta run. Can't wait to tell you everything! Say hi to everyone for us! Love Steph

3 MISERABLE IN THE CITY OF JOY

I t must be 100 degrees in here! Can't we get a fan? I think I'm going to pass out. Whose idea was this trip again? And what is that smell?"

These were some of the profound thoughts running through my head on my first day in India. I guess I had assumed I would be inspired by the natural beauty, excited about exploring and looking forward to tasting some local cuisine. But instead, all I could think of was how awful I felt.

Besides the obscene jet lag of ten and a half hours of time difference, the heat and humidity were making me nauseous, and we'd just landed an hour earlier. How, I wondered aloud, was I going to get through the next forty days like this? I was suddenly dizzy from a combination of heat, fatigue, the beginnings of a severe culture shock, and sleep-deprivation.

I'm sure my whining on the very first day did not bode well for Miriam, my friend and traveling buddy. If she was annoyed, though, she didn't show it. In fact, she was a rock for me the entire time. Five years her senior, I had fully expected to be the one encouraging and supporting her when the going got tough in India. But pretty much without exception, it was she who saw *me* through some very difficult days.

As I would soon discover, those weeks in India would be the most emotionally trying times in my life. I think my difficulties had a lot to do with feeling insecure or unsafe, and not being in control. I like life to be predictable, to feel that I have a handle on things. Little did I know when we were leaving Ottawa, and excitement filled every fiber of my body, that those forty days and nights would be anything but predictable.

I just felt so lost. It was hard at times to keep from freaking out. I know this sounds dramatic, but it's true. Some days I was convinced that if I didn't get on a plane that very day and head straight for home, something disastrous would happen. I don't know what I thought that disaster might be, but I was left with a feeling of ongoing anxiety just below the surface.

∗ ∗ ∗

When I set foot for the first time on Indian soil, something wasn't quite right. Yes, there was the wall of humidity and the pungent smell of something burning, and my churning stomach didn't help. But that wasn't it. Something was seriously wrong with me and I knew it from the first moment.

"Forty days." I said aloud. "Forty days until I can get back on a plane and go home."

Miriam looked at me and her face fell. I must have looked ashen, because she took my hand and began what would become her vigil of comfort and reassurance to me. Me! Who had so recently gushed to everyone back home about the great time we would have in India, about how many lives we would touch, and how we would say hello to Mother Teresa on their behalf. I had been such an ass. No. What really happened was that Miriam carried me throughout the trip and I know I would have thrown in the towel without her help. I was humbled to discover that at every turn, every snag, any little wrench in the works, I was thrown on my ear. I don't think a day went by while in India that I didn't question, complain to God, or try to bargain.

Why, God? Why?

Why did I have to come here?

Couldn't you have picked a cooler country?

Can you make something happen so that I can go home early?

I just want to go home. Who knew you could be this miserable in a place called the City of Joy?

4 SO SARI

As I mentioned in one of those early letters to Margie, on one of our first days in Cochin, Miriam and I rode in a little motorized rickshaw taxi with one of the sisters to a textiles shop to purchase saris. I chuckled to myself as I was reminded of the Schwarzenegger movie *Total Recall*. The taxis in that sci-fi world were strikingly similar to these, although the drivers in the movie were automated robots . . . but I digress.

In our rickshaw taxi, we sipped mango juice from drink boxes with little straws. It was the first time I had tried mango juice and I did not like it. I later looked in vain for apple juice, orange juice—even pineapple, but no luck. Mango seemed to have cornered the market. But more than any juice, because of the unbelievably humid and oppressive heat, bottled water had to be our constant companion. We had to have some kind of consistent hydration, as there was always a risk of foreigners becoming ill from dehydration.

It seemed that wherever we went in India that is how people referred to us: foreigners. It wasn't a derogatory term, just a description that meant we were not from this place, as if anyone needed to be told this. One look at our pale whiteness must have spoken loudly that we were not native to India. There we were, a couple of tallish, blond, pale-skinned young women who drew stares and the close attention of many a native passerby.

In fact, the first time I ventured out in public proudly wearing my newly acquired silk sari, I received an unexpected lesson in Indian culture: they are not shy to reach out and touch. A group of about twenty women, who were outside on a break from a sewing class at a community center, approached me, smiling and chatting. Then, I noticed, they looked determined. First, one woman touched my sari, holding out the long end of it to admire it. Then, another was feeling my hair, and another my earrings. I guess I was something of a novelty and it was show-and-tell time. They turned me around and around, chatting excitedly to one another in their own language, taking great pleasure in me. I didn't like it. What I didn't realize is that they were tickled at the unusual way I had donned my sari. Also, evidently my handiwork needed some tweaking.

A flurry of arms came at me and they had me unraveled and redressed again in about thirty seconds. It's funny now, to remember, but at the time I was unnerved and unsure of what to do. My face must have given me away because Miriam, who had apparently assembled her sari successfully, stood nearby, laughing hard. Seeing her face let me know that everything was okay. Once again, Miriam's undaunted joy reminded me that all was well. God had matched me with just the right person, given my growing unease. She was kind, funny, and so laid back. Most days, I was kept from taking things too seriously thanks to her calm manner and corny jokes, which she would endlessly try to explain if I didn't laugh as hard as she had thought I should. Obviously, she would say, I didn't get the joke.

One day, as we drove through a rural area, Father John took us to see a small silk factory. It seemed to be in the middle of nowhere. There, several dozen local women dressed in simple saris spun silk into exquisite textiles. There were shiny jewel tones, muted pastels and bold patterns, all bordered in gold or silver. Their machines looked ancient, but the workers were obviously skilled. The work they turned out was stunning. Then our tour guide brought us up to the roof where zillions of silkworms were drying in the sun. It was fascinating to see, and although the worms were clearly dead, I got the heebie-jeebies and didn't stay up there for long. I excused myself and headed back downstairs, starting to feel itchy. Outside the factory was a small body of water, like a canal or river. A warm breeze slowly moved the long strands of trees that looked a bit like weeping willows, their ends dipping into the water.

On the way home we bought fresh, local pineapples. The butter-soft, bright yellow flesh was so exquisite that once again I wondered what the heck kind of pineapples I'd been eating all my life back in Canada.

Meanwhile, my letters to Margie remained a lifeline. I told her everything that was happening to me in India.

Dear Margie,

I'm writing to you right now because I am overwhelmed and I know you'll understand. Miriam went out with Father John for the afternoon and I just spent eight hours with a priest and two nuns who spoke nothing to one another but their language, constantly. I tried to inject little things when I could, and they spoke English for a minute or two and then switched back. So I was just sitting there, pretty much staring at the wall. I thought I'd scream! I couldn't leave because I had no idea where we were; two sisters and I had taken a taxi and two buses to go visit this priest at his parish. We were there to help him decorate the altar for a festival the next day. We covered the entire altar with rolls of white paper, which seemed to take hours, and then they had me cover it with colored sequins of all shapes and sizes. I glued each one on individually. The three of them debated enthusiastically for a long while over which color streamers to put on, how high or low to hang them, whether they should add fringe, and so forth. They settled on a fuchsia theme. The whole thing was over the top as far as my own personal taste was concerned, but to each their own. Finally, we came in from the church to the priest's residence to have lunch.

Some of the strong, unfamiliar smells of their food turn me right off. This tends to decrease the appetite. They gave me two pieces of chicken, which I had happened to notice had been sitting on the counter for about four hours. When I said no thanks, they said it had been prepared especially for me. Despite my multiple polite attempts at declining, they insisted. I nibbled on a few bites and just couldn't stomach them. I ate a little bit of rice and drank some water but ultimately had to tell them my stomach was upset so they would stop offering me food! It's nice to be cared for but I felt like I wanted to punch something. Luckily, earlier in the week I had learned their word for enough: madi. So when I said it, they were pleasantly surprised that I knew it and they dropped the subject.

After lunch they asked if I'd like to lie down and I gratefully accepted, glad to be alone for a while. They showed me a sort of sofa in Father's office, and although it was made of wood, there was a puffy mint green throw pillow, which, once propped under my head, did the trick. I wasn't ill, just bored and a bit irritated with the whole situation. From the bookshelf beside me, I picked out a book called <u>Song of the Bird</u> by Anthony DeMello, an Indian author. It was a collection of stories about contemplative prayer, finding God within, etc., like parables. It really spoke to me.

On the way home while looking for a taxi in a busy area, I asked Sister Carmel if we could find somewhere to make a phone call so I could call my Mom. Shaking her head, she said that I'd have to pay cash up front and it would be very expensive. She basically was saying no, though not unkindly. She told me I could make the call later from the Center where we were staying and save money. I guess I just needed to talk to my Mom, or I felt powerless, or both. My face flushed and I knew if I blinked hot tears would spill out and roll down my cheeks. I held it together a while, but when we were settled in the taxi, Sister Carmel caught sight of my face. "You look sad," she said. "Just tired," I replied, smiling a little. And that was it. I was done chatting. I turned and looked out the window.

The rest of the day I had a very hard time smiling and carrying on much in the way of conversation, which was not easy. They always want to chat. It was a difficult day. Sometimes I just want to go home.

This place is so bizarre in every way—the food, the smells, the language, the animal sounds, the Muslim chanting loudly at 5 in the morning, the smoke and smog, the people staring at us all the time—everything! I'm letting it all hang out with you in this letter because I know I can and because I have to. It's 5 pm and Miriam will be out till 8 or 9 pm. I miss her. I thought I'd be fine without her for a while, but I have a feeling we are each other's lifeline. Well—she's mine, at least. If I were here without a friend from home I'd be having a much harder time.

Anyway, I'd better run. It's getting late and we have to get up early tomorrow. Hope all is well back home! I'll call soon.

Love Steph

I needed Miriam in India, and I needed to know that Margie was there for me, too, at home. I kept writing to Margie, and sometimes I was more upbeat!

Dear Margie,

Today is our last day in Cochin for a while. Tomorrow, Wednesday, Jan 17, we leave for Calcutta by train at 4:30 pm (which is 6 am Wednesday for you). It should take about three days! We'll call as soon as we arrive. It may take a little while to find a phone and arrange to call so don't worry if you don't hear from us. This week has been . . . memorable. It's been challenging in many ways, but I wouldn't trade it. And we are succeeding in losing weight without even trying! Neither of us has been sick so that's a bonus. Lately we've been preparing our own meals because we don't always like what they are serving. We eat mostly rice, veggies, and some chicken. And bananas—they are a staple at every meal. As you know, I hate bananas, but these ones are so fresh and sweet, they're almost bearable. When we get back here to Cochin after our time in Calcutta, we're going up to "the hills" where apparently some of the native peoples have never seen white people! I haven't seen any elephants yet, but Miriam said she saw 6 or 7 on the road the other day. I hope I get to ride one!

Take care. I miss you.

Love Steph

5 TRAINING

With one week in India under our belts, it was time to head off to the next part of our big adventure: the 48-hour, 1500-mile cross-country journey by train that would take us to Calcutta. Father John saw us off and we boarded an ancient mammoth of a railcar.

It was packed. Luckily, Father had booked us a berth—a teeny tiny area where we could sit and pull a curtain across, so we weren't on full display to the endless stream of travelers as they boarded or departed at the numerous stops and stations. But there we were: two eager twenty-somethings from snowy Canada, enormous packs on our backs, in t-shirts and long pants. We had been told not to wear shorts in India as they were considered immodest. Whistles were blowing, bells were ringing, and our excitement was growing. A man standing in the open doorway was yelling, at the top of his lungs, presumably something like "All aboard!" As we started inching forward there was a high-pitched screeching noise, like metal on metal, which settled down once things got moving. Soon the train hit its stride, rhythmically rocking us back and forth.

I felt giddy—high on life, charged up with that crazy fearlessness of youth. The berth was a cramped space that would be our seats by day and our beds by night. Our seats faced each other, so close that our knees almost touched. When it came time to sleep, I unhooked a very narrow, slightly padded bench and pulled it down, so it laid flat across our seats, spanning the berth. That would be my bed. From the wall above us we then unhooked and pulled down the upper bench—Miriam's bed.

To pass the time on the train, we read to each other, played cards, and braided one another's hair. We drenched our heads with hairspray, our hairdos becoming almost solid so we wouldn't need to brush or wash our hair for the duration of those two days and nights. We called them our helmets. We also slept, listened to our Sony Walkmans, strolled up and down the halls, and generally watched the world go by.

We would regularly hoist our packs onto our laps to rummage for something to eat. We'd packed peanut butter, honey, some bread, bananas, mango juice drink boxes, and a big bag of hard candies. But you can only eat so much of that stuff before you start feeling sick. The constant rocking didn't help, either. We journaled, wrote postcards, napped, and just stared out the window, trying to imagine what lay ahead for us in Calcutta.

There were long stretches when we didn't talk at all, passing the time playing hundreds of games of tic tac toe. Those hours held so much for us: restlessness, absurdity, fear, enjoyment and wonder . . . always wonder. We were silent, stupefied as the sun and moon took their turns coming and going as we passed tiny villages, dusty battered old train stations, and great huge expanses of lush unspoiled terrain dotted with tropical trees and peculiar countryside.

At every stop, seemingly every hour, day and night, someone would come on board hollering, "CHAI! CHAI! CHAI! CHAI! CHAI!" He would move from person to person, deftly pouring the steaming liquid from a big metal bucket with a handle and a spout as he walked up and down the aisle. The first time I heard it, shaken out of a very deep sleep, I thought I must have been dreaming. I could not make out what he was saying. It sounded like he was saying *Chaiahhh!* He just kept shouting it over and over. I came to hate those stops, with their abrupt awakenings. I never got used to them. I did try the Chai once though, and it was so sweet I could only stand the first sip. After that I had to make my way to the little bathroom down the hall to dump the rest of it away.

What can I say about that bathroom? Miriam was the first to experience it. When she returned, after a few minutes, she looked like she'd seen a ghost. "What is it?" I asked. "What's wrong?" She shook her head, trying to work out what to say. "I think I've been traumatized," she said. "Whaaa?" She had my attention. With a little impish grin, "I can't . . . you have to go see it for yourself," she said, shaking her head, "Tell me!" I insisted. But she wouldn't. She just pointed down the hall. "Go! I dare ya." I headed down the hall, the train jostling me back and forth, always back and forth. I looked in the bathroom, at first, but didn't see much. There was . . . just . . . a big hole in the floor, open right through to the tracks below. With only the guidance of a couple of big footprints—kind of like clown shoes—with one on either side of the hole, and a metal bar to hang onto, we were expected to take care of business on that very bumpy, sometimes lurching, fast-moving train. Miriam and I both felt that every time we used the facilities (which was a lot, over two days and nights) we should utter the words, "Sorry, India!" We looked forward to getting to Calcutta, anxious to find somewhere to grab a shower and hose down our sandals.

By the time we were an hour from Howrah Station in Calcutta, our final destination, getting nervous for whatever awaited us, we decided to stretch our legs and get a change of scenery. Making our way through the cars, we came to the very last one. Up ahead of me, Miriam peeked into an open door. Turning to me, she momentarily squeezed her eyes shut. Then, shaking her head, she mouthed, "Seriously?" I caught up to her and she stepped aside so I could see into the room. There it was: a bathroom. A regular bathroom, with a regular toilet and a sink with running water.

At some of the stops, when travelers would be getting off and coming on, people would lean into my berth, sometimes sitting for a second, albeit through the curtain, right onto my lap! From the train we saw endless rice fields, rugged terrain with all kinds of mountains and valleys, endless pristine plains, animals at large just hanging out at each of the stops—primarily monkeys. People in dirty clothes stood outside grass huts watching the train go by. Some smiled and waved. Some just looked, with a casualness that felt unusual to me.

Kids often ran along beside the tracks, some getting so close that my heart was in my mouth as they ran. They never seemed to get hurt, however. They seemed to know just how close they could get to the railcars without being in danger. That was one consistent thing during our time there: many of the children seemed unafraid; they were bold and confident beyond their years. I imagine this mild hubris served them well when trying to scrape together something to bring home to their family or to support themselves on the street.

I had known we would see poor communities in India— of course we would. I had seen scores of documentaries on poverty, read stacks of books about Mother Teresa and her people. Back home in Ottawa, I had worked at all four men's homeless shelters and at that time I was with Ottawa Innercity Ministries, leading teams of volunteers on street outreach in downtown Ottawa. I knew all about the poor . . . North American poor, that is. But this was India. We were coming face-to-face with a whole different kind of poverty.

It was such a strange period, the time spent on that train. Of course, it was special, unusual and rich . . . all that good stuff. But it was also evoking a kind of shadowy loneliness in me. I'm not sure how else to put it. Passing by so, so many decaying pockets of poverty, and seeing with my own eyes the endless string of huts and hearts, long since surrendered to their desolate lots—this was a poverty I hadn't known existed.

I found myself waking up to something that I wished I hadn't.

6 NO ROOM AT THE "Y"

After forty-eight hours on the train, sleep-deprived and hungry, Miriam and I finally arrived in Calcutta.

A nice older couple on the train had told us that cab drivers would be aggressive and try to overcharge us, and that we absolutely should not pay more than forty rupees. We thanked them and resolved to be strong. Then, carried by the momentum of all the travelers suddenly pushing us from behind, we oozed out of the train into a great undulating mass of people where everyone seemed to be yelling. I felt dizzy.

A big guy in the crowd caught my eye, and hollered, "Come! Come! I'll help you get to the taxis!" He beckoned for us to follow him. We did, and he cleared a path for us to get through the crowd. Then he pointed us toward the taxicabs. We thanked him for his help and turned to walk away. He started calling after us, not quite so friendly this time. It hadn't occurred to us that he expected a tip. We gave him some money, thanked him again and turned our attention to finding a cab. Suddenly it was wall-to-wall cab drivers coming at us, pushing each other aside, hollering numbers. "One hundred fifty! One hundred eighty!" We shook our heads, saying, "Forty!" They just laughed. They kept shouting numbers, each one louder than the last. We continued to stand firm at forty. But no one would to take us for forty. They all kept shouting higher numbers at us and we kept walking away, still saying, "Forty, forty." It was bizarre. Finally, one guy said okay to forty. Success! Or so we thought.

We put our bags in his open trunk and he slammed it shut as we climbed in the back seat. Then the driver promptly walked away and kept on going. For about five minutes we couldn't see where he had gone, then we spied him way down the street chatting with some other drivers. Tired and fed up, we got out, grabbed our stuff out of the trunk and went to find another cab. We walked right past our driver and he hardly glanced at us. After that, no one would take us for forty. It was a game.

Then another driver came along and said he would take us for forty. We accepted and followed him. He showed us to the same cab we had been in before. Looking at each other, we shrugged and said to each other, "Whatever," and put our stuff in the trunk once again. We also got in the cab again, and again he didn't start the car. We sat there while he picked up his newspaper.

We said, "We want to go now!"

"Now?" he said. "Oh, well it's one hundred and twenty to go now."

We looked at each other, threw the doors open, and jumped out. Miriam opened the trunk and we schlepped our bags out for a second time and took off the other way. By this time, I was on the verge of tears. "This is ridiculous!" I shrieked. The driver caught up to us, saying, "Okay, okay—forty to take you right now." We were so tired and hungry and just wanted to get safely where we were going. So we got into the cab for a third time. Finally, we were really on our way.

The cab darted in and out of traffic. We reached our destination in no time flat. We paid the man forty rupees, got our bags from the trunk, and the cab sped off. And there it was: the YM/YWCA nearest Mother Teresa's convent, the place where her volunteers usually stayed. Some friends who had made the same journey the previous year had told us not to worry, that there was usually plenty of space.

We climbed the very steep flight of stairs to the office, our massive backpacks threatening to throw us off balance. When we asked about a room, the man behind the desk told us that they were all booked up but he could get us in after February 5th. My jaw hung open. Miriam told him we were only in Calcutta until February 2nd. "And you didn't think to reserve ahead?" he said. We just stood there looking at him, shaking our heads. I felt stupid. He rolled his eyes and shook his head, making no attempt to hide his reaction. Tears filled my eyes and I prayed silently: *Oh, my dear God—do something. We are homeless, hungry, and alone at night in Calcutta.*

Maybe it sounds overly dramatic, but I really was frightened. Squeezing my shoulder blades together, I shook the straps of my backpack off my shoulders. It hit the floor with a huge thud, and I felt like doing the same. Then the man said there was a place he could call for us—a guesthouse a few blocks away, although he was making no promises. He motioned to a row of chairs along the wall, and we sat down. He made the phone call.

I noticed the wall behind the man at the desk. There was a big portrait of Jesus, one of my favorite images. I have the same picture at home. Feeling reassured, I sort of felt like God was saying: *Remember me? I'm still with you, you know. I've got this. You can trust me.*

The man put down the receiver and said we were in luck! Lee Memorial Mission Guesthouse had agreed to take us for one night. Miriam and I smiled at each other, thrilled that things were looking up. We stood up and hugged. I looked at the picture again and hoisted my burden onto my shoulders yet another time. We of course had no idea how to get there, but the man, now looking at us kindly, told us not to worry. He asked one of his employees to go along and show us the way. The young fellow stepped out from behind the counter, gave us a shy smile, and headed down the stairs. We followed.

By this time, it was really dark. He briskly walked ahead of us, quietly leading us through the streets of Calcutta. Music was blaring somewhere, and we passed a big group of men laughing and shouting, standing around a big fire. They took notice of us as we passed, a couple of them stepping out of the circle, smiling, looking us up and down. It was really creepy. Miriam and I moved closer and linked arms the rest of the way. I think it was less than a ten-minute walk but seemed to take forever. Finally, our guide stopped on the sidewalk and gestured toward the dusty two-story yellow building before us, Lee Memorial Mission. We thanked him profusely and Miriam rummaged in her fanny pack for a tip, but he just shook his head and headed back into the night.

As we approached the guesthouse, a very thin, very old man appeared at the front gate. He smiled and waved. "Welcome, girls! Come in." Although it was late it was still warm, he was all bundled up in a sweater, a burgundy knitted cap and scarf. He told us to call him Uncle. After a bit of small talk, he led us up the stairs to our room. On the landing toward the guest rooms, there was a portrait of Jesus—the very same one we had just seen at the Y. Uncle said that Miss Lee, the superintendent (who was also his niece), was out so he couldn't say yes to more than one night yet.

We were just happy to be there. Closing the door behind us, we flopped onto our beds, supremely happy to be settled and safe. I felt like we'd won the lottery. The room was huge like my living room, dining room, and kitchen area all together at home, with six beds, two big old armoires, two bathrooms, a shower, a ceiling fan, a desk and chair, and thankfully, doors that locked. All around the room there were inspirational Christian posters that said things like: "You will be blessed when you go out and come in." "Find a way, or make a way." And "I have made you, I will not forget you." That last one really touched me because it felt like another little reminder that God was there and an assurance that we were going to be okay.

By this point we were famished. We hadn't eaten much on the train besides the few things we'd bought in Cochin, and though we really were not keen to head out in the dark again, we had to eat. So we went downstairs to look for Uncle, hoping he could suggest a restaurant. Miss Lee had returned, and her uncle introduced us, telling her we'd been sent over from the Y. She raised an eyebrow, looking at Miriam and then me.

"You came to the city with nothing booked? And now you want to stay here?" she said. We just shrugged and smiled lamely.

She looked at Uncle and mumbled something we couldn't hear. He inspected his sweater and started removing lint. Miss Lee sighed and looked down at her ledger, over the top of her glasses. She scanned it, turned a few pages back and forth, and said, "You may stay here tonight. Tomorrow you'll need to find somewhere else."

She called one of her staff, a man who lived next door and asked him to show us to a good clean restaurant. He appeared within minutes. He seemed delighted to meet us and eager to help despite the hour. We walked close behind him for about five minutes, making our way again through all the people, rickshaws, and stalls. Finally, we reached the Golden Dragon Chinese restaurant. Intoxicating smells wafted out onto the street. I was giddy, eager to get eating. We thanked our guide repeatedly and said goodbye, but he shook his head and simply said, "I'll wait." We told him it was okay to leave, that we would find our way back. But he just smiled and repeated, "I'll wait." So we asked him to join us. But he just stood there on the sidewalk.

Miriam and I looked at each other, feeling guilty, but we had to eat. We reluctantly went in and turned our attention to the menu, ordering chicken chow mein, fried rice, and spring rolls. The piping hot dishes arrived a few minutes later and we absolutely chowed down. And we ordered Coke. I had started to crave it since we'd arrived in India. And though it had only been a few weeks since we'd had it, on this night it was a liquid luxury. As we delighted in our feast, Miriam and I agreed that the best Chinese food we had ever tasted could be found right there in India.

Here's a letter I sent home from Calcutta:

Dear Margie,

Although we are in the dirtiest, scariest city in the world, I feel we have little to fear but fear itself, which of course continues to be a contender. But I'm learning to face the fear and turn it over to God more and more, although it's easier some days than others. Sometimes I feel like I have a big glass bubble around me, like nothing can touch me. Other days, I'm terrified of everything and just wish I was home. In any case, this place has changed me and I'm sure it will continue to do so for a long time to come. I feel so much more alive these days—so much more full of feeling and caring for everyone I see. I could go on forever, but

I'm already running out of paper. Will you please keep my
letters? I'd like copies for my journal when I get back. Got
to go find somewhere to buy stamps and mail this letter.
We miss you!
Love Steph (weary but happy in Calcutta)

Everything I was encountering in Calcutta felt new to me, some of it scary, some of it exhilarating. There was the music, the array of bold colors, the scents (both sweet and not-so-sweet), the exotic animals, the strong and unusual tastes, the crazy humidity, and on and on. Then there was the peculiar, haunting, early morning drone somewhere in the distance that woke us one morning. Peering out our open window across the hazy dawn, I was at first perplexed, unable to work out what it was. Only later did I learn that it was the Muslim call to prayer.

There was the quiet wonder that filled me as I sat alone at dusk, the white glow of a perfectly round little moon hanging in a lavender sky. The heat was thick and moist. Sometimes it felt like inhaling steam. I often felt nauseous and dizzy. Some days I had to take a couple of cold showers just to keep the queasiness at bay. And of course, there were numerous things we could not safely eat as they had been washed in local water. I had never needed to be so vigilant about my money, careful to keep it hidden in a belt under my clothes. It occurred to me many times that I had had it pretty good back in Canada. At home while in hospital, I'd never had to ask the nurse taking my blood not to re-use the needle she had just used on the previous patient, as I did when I got sick in India. There were so many unknowns.

Miriam and I kept laughing. We elbowed each other when something struck us as absurd or incongruous. We giggled at stupid things that weren't actually that funny. We mercilessly poked fun at each other over dinner.

7 UNCLE FRANK

Next to meeting Mother Teresa, the best thing about the trip for me was meeting Frank Lee. Uncle, as he told us to call him, was kind and welcoming. At a time when we were scared, exhausted, and badly needed a break, he had taken us in. He had welcomed us without hesitation, even though the guesthouse was almost at capacity, risking the disapproval of his niece, the manager. Apparently, she had told him he was not to accept any more guests until others had left. But Miss Lee was out when our call came from the Y, and, as he would later explain to her, he just couldn't say no.

When we returned from dinner on our first night in Calcutta, Uncle brought us up to our room and the three of us went in. Closing the door behind him, he reported that Miss Lee had also returned. Apparently, she was unhappy with him, but with a little smile he told us not to worry, that he knew she would come around. She had said we could stay there that night but that we'd have to find somewhere else the next day. But leaning in close to us, in a half-whisper, looking at Miriam and then me, Uncle said, "Okay. Here's what we're going to do. Tomorrow morning, go out and don't come back till suppertime. When you return, tell Miss Lee you tried everywhere but you were unsuccessful. She'll have no choice but to let you stay! Then, repeat the same thing each day and with any luck I will get to be your host for your entire stay in Calcutta." Gleefully, he then added, "Isn't that a great plan?"

Miriam and I looked at each other and smiled. It was a great plan. And it worked just as he had said, although I'm pretty sure she caught on after the third day or so because that's when she stopped asking us to leave. Besides, Uncle seemed to have a soft spot for us from the very first day and I suspect he'd buttered her up and brought her around.

One day, Miss Lee quietly mentioned to us that her Uncle would be celebrating his 91st birthday the following day. She could see that the three of us had become fast friends and thought we would want to know. She was right. Then Miriam, suddenly excited, blurted out: "We'll get a cake!" Miss Lee smiled and shook her head a little, raising a hand. Undaunted, Miriam spoke again before Miss Lee could say anything. "Please let us do it! It will be our gift to him, our way of thanking him for taking care of us." Miriam glanced my way and with her eyes, told me to say something. I piped up. "Yes! We insist." Miss Lee smiled a little smile. "Well, if it will make you happy, that would be lovely." She took a little square of paper from a desk drawer and wrote down the name and address of a good bakery.

The next day, once dismissed from our morning of volunteering at Mother Teresa's orphanage, we grabbed a quick bite. As we did most days, we ate lunch at the Blue Sky Cafe, a great little spot for tourists, not too far from Mother Teresa's house. We ate fries and drank Coke in glass bottles. Then we set off in search of a birthday cake for Uncle. Though we hadn't realized it, the route we had mapped out took us right through the slums. We had been joking around and chatting until that point. But then, looking around us at the picture of poverty before us, we lowered our voices. Soon we just walked in silence.

We were walking past impossibly tiny dwellings, each one crammed up against the next. Some of them resembled the old shed in my parents' back yard, if that shed had been repeatedly broken and reassembled with various other materials and left for years to rust. These were families' actual homes. When we were volunteering, we had helped out in a place that was set up to serve the poor, where, in a flurry of happy activity, we knew what to do and where we belonged. But here in this place, it was clear that Miriam and I didn't belong. It was a whole other little world and it felt like we were trespassing.

We dodged dirty puddles, small random piles of garbage, and the occasional dead rodent. Oh—and the smell . . . always there was that smell, wherever we went, like burning garbage and tires. There was no escaping it. And there were so many people. Women were hanging laundry on ropes strung between trees or posts and cooking over open fires. Kids and dogs came and went. And there were babies—literally crawling in the dirt. It was just like those TV shows we had seen back home, the ones making appeals for the poor people in developing countries. I felt extremely uncomfortable, like a voyeur.

We kept moving forward and I tried not to look anyone in the eye. It was no wonder Mother Teresa had called them the poorest of the poor. We walked a little more and, following our map, turned a corner. Then, just like that, it was behind us. We came to a busy main artery and stood there a moment, taking in the dizzying array of activity before plunging in. Then we were off again. Out of nowhere, several taxi cabs and rickshaws slowed up beside us as we walked, each calling out to us over and over:

"Sister! Sister! Need a ride?" the drivers called. We declined. Repeatedly.

They kept hollering, until finally they gave up and disappeared into the fray. I'm not sure why people often called us sister. I wondered whether everyone assumed we were nuns, or if it was just a thing they said, the way men are sometimes called uncle.

Before long we found the bakeshop. We bought a little round chocolate cake and asked them to write, "Happy Birthday Uncle" on it. They did so with bright yellow icing. We also bought two number candles: 9 and 1.

Back at the guesthouse, we found everyone at home: Uncle, Miss Lee, the housekeeper, and the man who had taken us to the Chinese restaurant that first night. They were all in the sitting room, casually chatting. Miss Lee looked at us, then at the little box Miriam was holding. Miss Lee turned to the housekeeper and spoke to her quietly. Uncle didn't notice; he was too busy oohing and aahing over the bright colored silk saris we had bought in the bazaar earlier.

Miriam excused herself and slipped from the room. The housekeeper reappeared, carrying a tray with a big pot of tea, some cups, plates, forks and little white paper napkins. She set it down on the coffee table in front of Frank.

"What's all this?" he asked, looking up at her.

Then, from the hallway, a loud, happy voice started singing: "HAPPY BIRTHDAY, TO YOU!"

Miriam appeared in the doorway, holding the cake with the number candles lit. We all joined in the singing, everyone smiling. Frank sat there looking utterly shocked. He looked around the circle, his brow furrowed, trying to work out what was going on. He looked up at Miriam, who had brought the cake over to him and held it out so he could see it.

"What's this all about?" he said.

Miriam had arranged the numbers as 19 instead of 91. She began, with a smile: "You're too young to be turning 91. Today you're 19."

Uncle Frank looked down at his lap and for a second everyone was quiet. When he looked up again, his eyes were glistening. With a shy smile, he looked up and then blew out his candles. Everyone cheered and clapped. "You girls," he said, slowly shaking his head. "You have no idea what this means to me. . . ." Then we all had something in our eyes, and I'm pretty sure even Miss Lee wiped a tear away. Frank let out a little laugh and kept repeating, "I had no idea! No idea!"

Uncle Frank eventually stood up, reached out, and hugged the two of us around our necks, pulling us in so close that Miriam and I almost kissed. The housekeeper started pouring the tea as Miss Lee cut the cake. Later, in our room, Miriam and I talked about how we were so surprised at his reaction. It had been such a simple gesture. Wasn't it just the usual thing to do when someone has a birthday, to get them a cake? But it struck a chord for him. Maybe it had been a while since he'd had a birthday cake. It was the least we could do for our doting guardian angel. He seemed to delight in everything we did. It was the kind of rare friendship that finds its footing right away and we were starting to dread saying goodbye just a few days later. Frank and I exchanged a few letters in the months after I had returned home from India. In one letter, I thanked him again for taking care of us that first night in Calcutta. Here's what he wrote back:

Dear Stephanie,
you don't need to thank me for what I was able to do for both of you that night regards accommodation. It was God that sent you to the right place to meet the right person. He is a Loving Father who cares for his children. Place all

your faith and trust in HIM and all will be taken care of by HIM. I will now shut up as it is 2:10 am. Somehow my sleep won't come.

Bye, God Bless You and Protect You always. You two children are always in my nightly prayers.

Yours Sincerely,

Frank (Uncle)

In his last letter to me a few months later, he wrote:

Stephanie, I believe God brought us together. I believe that, too.

8 CULTURE SHOCK

I lay in my lumpy bed, slowly awakening to the sounds of early morning prayer chants as they filled the air. For a brief moment, I figured I must be dreaming some strange dream. The chants sounded like a bunch of long, loud moans blaring from a loudspeaker.

Through the metal grates on the windows I could see the dark sky. The beep-beep-beep of my travel alarm interrupted my sleep. I sat up, suddenly awake. My thoughts raced. What time is it? Ugh . . . it's 5 a.m. Where am I? Oh, right—Calcutta! Day two and counting.

The sprawling, drafty room seemed like something out of a Fifties sorority B movie: six single beds with metal frames with peeling, hospital-green paint, mismatched linens and faded beige walls. Miriam stirred and asked what time it was. Too early, I groaned. My complaint about the hour only lasted a moment, as we both started to stretch and make eye contact. Smiling broadly at each other, we chanted our mantra once again: "We're in India!" and then, "We're in Calcutta!" Although neither of us was fond of rising or shining, we both hopped out of bed and clutched each other, rejoicing like two little kids, gleefully waking up obscenely early on Christmas morning.

Skipping into the massive concrete bathroom, I turned on the faucet. Discovering only icy cold water raining down from the showerhead, I filled a metal bucket. Uncle had given us some kind of an element the night before; he said it was for heating up water for a sponge bath. The rusty metal appliance looked like the element inside of a stove, all coiled up with an electrical cord attached to it. There was a little hook for hanging it into the bucket of water. But hadn't we always been told that anything electrical was never to find its way anywhere near water? But here we were, about to plunge a bare piece of electric metal into water and then plug it in! I called Miriam in and asked whether she thought this a smart thing to do. Looking down at the bucket of water and then up at me holding the appliance and its cord, she just shook her head and backed away, leaving the room.

"No way. I'm not doing that!" she called from the bedroom. Uncle had sworn that this was a normal practice and perfectly safe, but we couldn't be sure. I put down the warmer far away from the bucket and decided that the shower couldn't be that cold. It was. Shrieking as the sub-zero water hit my quivering, goose-bumped body, Miriam came flying in, fearing I'd been electrocuted.

I hollered, "Stupid water, stupid bucket, stupid, stupid India!" jerking the faucet off. She turned and left the room, shaking her head and chuckling. I called out behind her, "Keep laughing, kiddo! Soon it will be your turn!"

Soaking and freezing cold, I dried my hands, picked up the banished appliance and dropped it into the bucket. "Here goes nothing!" I called out. "Nice knowing you!" Miriam appeared in the doorway, wincing. Bracing myself for God-knows-what, I thrust the plug into the wall. I screamed and jumped back; the fact that I was naked while doing it was the least of my worries. And then: nothing happened. Nothing, except that the terrifying appliance hummed a little as it presumably started to warm the water. Puffing out the breath she'd been holding, Miriam was laughing again. "I'm glad," I said, stifling a smile, "I'm providing you with such comic relief!"

I grabbed my towel to cover myself, waited for the water to warm and my heart to slow down. After Miriam had left the room for the third time, I shook my head, muttered some choice words, and grumbled. Kneeling down on the cold concrete and wetting my cloth in the now warmish water, I started to giggle. I laughed so much that Miriam called in to me and said, "Careful! You might shake that bad mood!" This only spurred me on and soon I was cackling at the idea of my naked self, kneeling there in front of the metal bucket, washing off the Calcutta soot.

9 FINDING MOTHER TERESA

I suppose eating chow mein from a street vendor in Calcutta is not the brightest thing I have ever done. We had been repeatedly warned to steer clear of fresh fruits and veggies—bean sprouts, in this case—as they had been washed in local water. Our North American gastrointestinal systems were likely to rebel against them, and until this particular day we had been careful to drink only bottled water.

One night, I remember how Miriam and I shared a look, and just kind of shrugged. What were we to do? It had been many hours since we'd eaten and we were ravenous. So when Uncle walked up to the vendor and ordered the chow mein, paid the man, and then happily handed each of us the steaming offerings, we didn't have the heart (or the stomach!) to refuse. It was served in makeshift bowls fashioned out of newspaper, lined with plastic wrap. Uncle watched with delight as we picked up our plastic forks and dug in. And let me say, it was scrumptious! And even though it was just about the yummiest thing we'd eaten so far in India, I had a niggling sense that we might come to regret it.

Of course, we hadn't come from Ottawa to Calcutta simply to eat chow mein.

Before long, Miriam and I were ready to make our way on foot to 54A Lower Circular Road—the Mother House of the Missionaries of Charity of Mother Teresa. Uncle had given us excellent directions, so off we went. He waved to us enthusiastically, hollering, "Have a good day! Don't come back till suppertime!"

What came at us in the next half hour was dizzying. The speed and volume of the cars were frightening, and the apparently optional traffic laws didn't help. Each car seemed to me to be pretty much identical to the next—all were dark in color with a style that looked like they belonged in my grandparents' photo album. But every car moved swiftly, noisily, and fearlessly along the main artery where we were walking.

The noise of the city with its horns, music, and vendors selling their wares—all mixed in my head as chaotic and deafening. In reality, it was the sound and life of the city itself—which at times could also be exciting, but unnerving.

Miriam and I walked quickly, chatting happily, pointing out this or that, whatever seemed interesting—which was everything. We had to dodge stray animals along the way—dogs, cats, monkeys, and the odd pig. And then, ambling along by the side of the road was a cow, possibly a sacred one. All of it somehow melted seamlessly into the fray.

After about half an hour of brisk walking, following Uncle's directions of rights, lefts, and short cuts, we finally found it: The Motherhouse. It was an old, plain, tired-looking, grey concrete, low-rise building. This, I thought to myself, is the home of Mother Teresa, the international headquarters of the Missionaries of Charity? I guess I had expected it to be at least a little bit pretty or stately, like some other convents I'd seen over the years. But of course, this was no ordinary convent, no ordinary kind of ministry. Mother Teresa and her sisters had taken a vow of poverty, among the poorest of the poor, so it made sense that their home would be a very humble one.

As we approached the front door, Miriam excitedly pointed to a small wooden "IN/OUT" sign on the wall, the kind you might see in an office. The little sliding door was covering the word OUT. "Steph!" Miriam said, "She's IN! Mother Teresa is IN!" Our eyes locked. Full on smiles, we could barely contain our glee. For months we had prepared for this, dreamed of this, hoped to find our hero at home. Now we were standing outside her front door, and she was in. My belly flipped and I regretted the chow mein. I think I held my breath as Miriam reached out to ring the bell.

Soon the door opened, and we were face-to-face with one of the Missionaries of Charity, our very first one. Sister Bethany wore a plain white sari with a couple of blue stripes around the edge, so familiar to us Mother Teresa enthusiasts. Miriam and I introduced ourselves and told her we were there to volunteer. Sister Bethany said we were most welcome and told us to come back at 5 p.m. to register. Then she invited us to go upstairs and take some quiet time in the chapel if we wanted to. We thanked her and headed up the stairs.

Halfway up, on the landing, we stopped to look at a big map of the world on the wall. Hundreds of little round colored pins were scattered all across it. A young volunteer who passed us on the stairs told us that visitors were invited to put a pin on the map to show where they came from. Canada was already crammed with pins. I ran my fingers over the little round balls that covered Ontario, and suddenly felt homesick.

Reaching the top of the stairs, Miriam and I approached the chapel, briefly pausing before going in. Taking off our sandals, we placed them neatly on the floor outside the door. Then we peered into the huge room, and, finding it empty, tiptoed in and sat down on the floor. The altar was across the room between the windows; a life-size crucifix hung on the wall. It was a beautiful, simple place, a sanctuary from the outside world. I was so glad to be there.

My shoulders ached from the heavy pack I had carried around so much. My nerves felt jangled and my chest was tight. I took a couple of deep breaths and tried to relax. A warm wave of emotion rose in my chest and then the tears came. I guess I was so relieved that we had finally made it there in one piece, and overjoyed that we were actually there in Mother Teresa's chapel—God's house.

Then something strange happened to me. I don't know how to explain it. . . . I just felt like God was filling me completely with pure love. That's the only way to say it: pure love. I wiped my wet face a bit with the black and white cloth tote bag I had bought in the bazaar earlier. Miriam slipped her arm around my shoulders and gave me a squeeze and a warm smile.

A few minutes later, a bell started ringing. One by one, the Missionaries of Charity filed in and kneeled down in tidy rows. Miriam and I looked at each other and figured this was our cue to leave. Scrambling to our feet, we made for the door, but at that moment, Mother Teresa appeared in the doorway. She looked toward us and smiled, beckoning for us to come closer as she knelt down just inside the door.

Silently, Mother Teresa gestured for us to kneel down and kind of mouthed that we'd chat later. Then, with an impish grin, she looked around evasively, as though she might get in trouble for talking. I stifled a chuckle, fearing I might laugh out loud. Miriam and I knelt down, looking at one another with a quiet intensity bordering on hysteria. Mother Teresa then handed each of us a rosary. Miriam turned to me and silently mouthed, "Oh. My. Gosh." I just sat there, still crying a little, but now cracking up too, shaking my head. This was really happening. We were hanging out with Mother Teresa.

There we were: two faithful Roman Catholics, praying the Rosary, with Mother Teresa. No big deal, right? We'd traveled to the other side of the world to work with the poor and if we happened to meet her or see her somewhere, so much the better. But this . . .

After we finished the communal prayers, the room was quiet for a few minutes except for the odd cough or the rattling of rosary beads. I glanced at Mother Teresa, trying to be nonchalant. Then, breaking the silence (and startling me), she patted the floor with two loud thumps. Suddenly, everyone was on their feet. Miriam and I looked at each other, jumping up once again.

The Missionaries of Charity strode out one-by-one, some of them turning to smile at us as they left. We smiled back.

We decided to sit back down on the scratchy burlap mat that covered the massive concrete floor. I must have been leaning back on the heel of my left hand before because a pattern of little squares had appeared on it. Realizing that Mother Teresa was still in the room, and that she might be waiting to talk to us, I was suddenly nervous. What do you say to a living saint? Taking a slow deep breath, I tried to stay calm. The fragrance of melted wax and blown-out wicks filled the air as someone snuffed out the candles. Something like burning car tires or roofing tar also filled my nostrils from the open windows, and the world outside, which brought in the sound of honking cars and sirens too.

I closed my eyes for a moment, smiling. How many times had I seen photos of this huge, sparse, beautiful upper room? I had wondered what it was like to be there with all the Missionaries of Charity, and of course with Mother Teresa. Then Miriam was gently nudging me.

"Steph," Miriam whispered in my ear, "Mother Teresa's calling us over. . . ." I felt my face flush.

Mother Teresa was right there, just a few feet away, waiting to talk to us. We hopped up and she motioned for us to follow her out into the hallway. Then, turning to us, she reached out, and taking our hands asked, "Where are you from, girls?"

We told her we were from Ottawa, Canada. She smiled and nodded slowly, as though recalling something. "Ah, yes . . . Ottawa. I have been there. What a beautiful city. You know, there are some other girls here from Canada. You will have to meet them." We nodded and smiled.

Then Mother asked, "Have you been to see the children at our orphanage down the street?" We shook our heads and told her we'd only just arrived. "Why don't you go there now?" she said. "Go spend time with them. You can come back later to get registered and meet some of the other volunteers. Then after supper, you're welcome to join us for Adoration of the Blessed Sacrament this evening. Will you come to Mass tomorrow morning at 6 a.m.?"

We told her we wouldn't miss it.

"That's good. Afterwards you can have some tea and bananas with the others. Then Sister will give you your assignments and send you off for the day. Goodbye for now, girls."

And with that, she smiled and bowed slightly to us with her hands clasped in front of her. Then she turned away and walked toward what I assumed were the offices. Soon she was flanked by other volunteers and some of her sisters, all chatty and gently vying for her attention.

We just stood there, watching, somewhat stunned. There was a kind of contagious, happy energy in the air as sisters went about the business of running things all around us.

Then Miriam turned to me and we clutched each other. With wide eyes and faces full of joy, we said to each other, "We met Mother Teresa!" Then we turned and flew down the stairs, full of nervous excitement. Not only had we found her at home, we got to meet her in person. And she even took the time to talk with us. I hadn't dreamed she would be so accessible, if she were even around at all. I would have been happy just to look across a room and catch a glimpse of her. But there Mother Teresa was: approachable, friendly, and human.

10 THE BODY OF CHRIST

*K*haligat, Home for the Dying Destitutes. Or *Nirmal Hriday*, Place of the Pure Heart. Whatever its name, it was the place where Mother Teresa first started looking after those who were close to death, who had no one else to take care of them. It didn't matter to me what they called it. I just knew I needed to go there. It was for this that I traveled across the world—this, and the hope of meeting the little woman herself. And I'll confess—I realize now—that the trip wouldn't have been quite as rich and rewarding had I not had the chance to meet Mother Teresa in person. In any case, I wouldn't trade those six weeks for anything. It didn't start out that way though.

A few years before the trip, I had participated in the Ottawa Hospital's palliative care training and became a volunteer. I was also involved in Camp Quality, a program for kids with terminal diseases, and found I had a comfort level with death and dying. I thought I had found my niche. So when I walked through the doors of the Home for the Dying Destitutes in Calcutta that first day, I fully expected to feel right at home. I figured I would fit right in and jump in wherever I was needed. It doesn't get much better than this, I thought to myself. Here I am, after all these years since I first sensed a calling to work with the dying, and I'm right in the thick of it!

But this wasn't going to be like any volunteering I'd done back home. The first person I saw was a very frail, elderly woman with papery, light brown skin. She lay there on a low cot, a couple of feet off the ground. I suspected she was close to death. Psyching myself up for a grueling yet fulfilling day, I rolled up my sleeves and strode toward her, determined to help.

Her thin fingers clutched a faded grey blanket. Drawing nearer, I could see that her eyes were closed and she was slowly turning her head back and forth. I wondered if she was in pain. What happened next still haunts me. A raspy noise filled my ears and then it hit me—it was her breathing. For a few moments, that rattling, gasping sound was all I could hear. I stood there stunned, unmoving. My knees buckled. That wretchedly painful, dying, breathing! My face got hot and a feeling of nausea washed over me. I thought I might faint. Air, I thought, I need air.

Stumbling back toward the door, I was suddenly afraid I might throw up. I tripped over a big doorstop and fell out onto the front steps, unhurt. There, outside this place I had dreamed about for many years, I panicked, my heart pounding in my ears. What was wrong with me?

"You okay kiddo?" I heard Miriam say from behind me, her voice startling me as I turned to let out the breath I'd been holding. She had noticed I didn't look well and came out to check on me.

Good question, I thought. I didn't have an answer. I nodded and managed a little smile. I mumbled, "I'll be okay. You go on ahead. I'll catch up." She flashed one of her disarming chill-out-everything-will-be-okay smiles at me, and I felt a little better.

Alone again on the front steps, I then tried to make myself go back in. Frustrated, I reminded myself that I'd just traveled halfway around the world to visit this place and I was wasting precious time. The orientation for new volunteers was under way. I was missing it and I wanted badly to be part of it. But at that moment I just could not go back in. It seemed so sad and dim, so concrete and full of pain. The strong smells of urine and bleach were also dizzying.

My thoughts raced: *What was it about this place of death that I had wanted so badly to see? Why had I felt so compelled to go all the way to India, only to have this happen?* I prayed . . . *God, what am I doing here? You called me to come, and here I am. But what's the use in being here if I can't even face the first person I see? What am I supposed to accomplish here if I don't even have the guts to stick it out? The heat here is making me sick, I don't like the food and I have no privacy. I want to go home.*

I was busy feeling very sorry for myself when I heard the small voice deep inside. *Trust me. Try again. You can trust me.* There was that gentle invitation again, to which I dutifully answered in my head: *No way. This place is a hellhole! I'm going*

*to find a diner and sit there drinking a Coke till Miriam is done
and ready to head back to the guesthouse.*

I started toward the door to go tell Miriam I was leaving
when the words niggled at me again. *Come on, Stephie. Give it
another chance. It will be okay. I am with you. Remember?*

I stopped a moment. I had heard and trusted that small voice
throughout my life, and I had to admit, I'd always been okay, one
way or another. God could be trusted. . . . And just then it hit
me—how could I not have realized it before? Six months earlier,
I had sat at my dear grandmother's bedside in the hospital. She
was dying and I knew it. Her breathing had become shallow and
a bit raspy. Hardly conscious now, her tiny frame moved her
chest slowly up and down under the sheet as she took each long,
slow breath. The rattling sound of it was difficult to listen to, but
I knew she would soon be at rest. The time between each breath
kept getting longer. Then, after we had kept vigil for several
hours, my dear Grandma Emmons drew her last breath. She just
. . . stopped. My Dad and I were right there when it happened—
he, at the foot of the bed, me at her side. One moment she was
there, and then the next, this special woman was just gone. It
was as gentle as that.

Just then, the loud honk of a car horn made me jump and
suddenly I was back in the present moment, back in Calcutta. I
sat there outside on the cement steps wiping away the tears and
it hit me: I realized that I was of course still grieving the loss
of my Grandma. It was no wonder I had such a strong reaction
when I saw that old woman. The sound of her breathing, the

sight of her frailty—it all brought me right back to that day the previous summer. I cried, and although I felt shaky and scared, I decided I would give it another shot. *Who knows*, I thought. *Maybe this encounter is all part of God's plan to help move me along in the grieving process.*

I took several slow, deep breaths, and started to feel better. My heart started to settle down, and a few minutes later I pushed the heavy wooden door and went back in.

The place seemed less scary and brighter somehow. Another volunteer had seen me duck out and walked over my way. Stacey was a lovely, petite, 19-year-old woman from Scotland who had traveled there alone to lend a hand for a while. She was helping people bathe. She gave me a warm smile and asked if I'd like to hang out with her until I felt more comfortable. I accepted, grateful not to have to face the woman who had reminded me of Grandma. I watched as Stacey lovingly approached a frail woman a few beds down. Gently, wordlessly, she encouraged her to come and be bathed. The language barrier made it necessary to use some creative communication, mostly very simple improvised sign language. The woman stirred slowly, her face wincing with pain as she struggled to her feet. With Stacey supporting her, the two walked slowly and carefully to the bathing area. I plodded along awkwardly behind them, not quite sure what to do. I really felt for the woman—this was not a private shower area, nor was it a comfortable one. It was a large room with concrete walls, benches, and several showerheads.

As we gingerly removed the woman's clothes, I did a double take. Her skeletal body was covered in open sores. She could scarcely stand without help. She shivered and wept quietly. So did I. Stacey had me drape a clean towel on the shower bench and then gracefully lowered the woman to a seated position and turned on the water. Picking up the hose and showerhead, she then tenderly washed her with warm water. It was a beautiful thing. But what really got me was the love with which this was done, the leisurely pace at which Stacey worked. Her unhurried manner helped the old woman to relax and allow herself to be cared for. It was as though they were the only two people on earth.

Looking about the large shower room, then, I saw this merciful act being repeated all around us. Several other women were being bathed and having their wounds dressed by a mosaic of volunteers from who knows where. One of the Missionaries of Charity came by with fresh, clean gowns for those being showered. I just stood there marveling, watching it all unfold.

Once she was dressed, we helped our friend back to bed and got her settled. One of the sisters gave her something for the pain and a few sips of cold water. Then Stacey fed her half a banana, one slice at a time. Our lady lay back gingerly on the sheet. I pulled the blanket up, tucked her in, and smiled. She smiled back, her face now relaxed, her eyes closing. With that, she drifted off for a peaceful rest. I huffed out a sigh, and a feeling of there's-nowhere-else-I'd-rather-be-right-now washed over me. My absorption in the beauty of these moments had caused me to entirely forget my own trouble. (Funny how that happens. . . .)

I excused myself to find the washroom. *Just think*, I said to myself, *you were about to bolt out of here like a scared rabbit! Think of what you would have missed.* Wow. *This day*, I mused, *would be something to take home and reflect on for a long time. This is what I came for; it doesn't get any better than this!* When I rejoined them, Stacey asked me to go back to the shower room and bring the wet towels to the laundry area. With a smile on my face and a spring in my step, I shook my head, smiling as I headed back to the showers, trying to take it all in. And then, I saw them. There—just beyond where we had bathed our dear lady. I hadn't noticed them before. On the concrete wall, painted in bold, capital letters were the words:

THE BODY OF CHRIST. Whoa.

The words of Jesus from Matthew's Gospel popped into my head: "Whatever you did for one of the least of these brothers and sisters of mine, you did for me." Maybe that's what Mother Teresa meant when she said that when they serve the poor they do it "with Jesus, for Jesus, to Jesus." He is ever-present in the distressing disguise of the poor, as she put it. Each and every one of them, of us—carries Jesus himself, because he dwells within. Mother also said, "We are touching Christ's body in the poor. In the poor it is the hungry Christ that we are feeding, it is the naked Christ that we are clothing, it is to the homeless Christ that we are giving shelter. It is not just hunger for bread or the need for clothes or of the homeless for a house made of bricks. Even the rich are hungry for love, for being cared for, for being wanted, for having someone to call their own."

After witnessing the people being bathed and looked after so affectionately, I didn't see the place as dim or depressing anymore. I saw cheerfulness, warmth, and tender care being offered by the Sisters and volunteers. It felt like a sacred place—holy ground, even. I learned a lot from that young volunteer, and she helped me by guiding me and showing me how I could make myself useful. I managed to finish my shift that first day and returned several times to that place of life and death, each time feeling more alive, at ease, and able to enter into the fullness of the experience.

"Because we cannot see Christ we cannot express our love to him; but our neighbors we can always see, and we can do for them what, if we saw him, we would like to do for Christ," Mother Teresa once said.

When I look back, I have a hard time believing I was even there. What could have possibly qualified me to go there? What was I thinking? I've wrestled with these questions for years, always unable to come up with an answer. But I kept on and on, bugging God, asking God to help me understand it all.

I'm not a nurse or even a medic, I'd tell him. *I don't work for the Red Cross or anything remotely like that.* I just felt called to go there (whatever that means), to show up and see how I might be of use. Recently, my friend Pauline told me about a line she had heard somewhere. It blew my socks off and has been helping me put some of my questions to rest: "He doesn't call the qualified," she told me. "He qualifies the called."

Another morning, after that first terrifying-then-holy one, after 6 a.m. Mass at the Motherhouse, a couple of the more seasoned volunteers reached out to me and Miriam. They invited us to meet up at day's end to hang out and talk. We gladly accepted.

So later that day, when our work was finished, we all gathered at the nearby bus stop as planned. There was a lot of chatter and swapping of the day's amazing moments on that long bus ride back as we debriefed. Some of us then made our way to the Blue Sky Cafe where volunteers often tended to congregate. Others headed back to their hotel or guesthouse to rest and unwind. I was reminded of that old show, *M*A*S*H*, when the medical personnel got together to play cards, have a drink, and blow off steam.

We all needed those times, those breaks from the madness of war. We needed a time-out from madness, too—the impossible human suffering we had touched and seen up close. We needed each other as touchstones, sounding boards, and people to just have fun and forget with, for a little while. We came from many backgrounds and countries. But on days like these, we were all the same. Nothing brings you to a common ground more than watching volunteers carry in a thin, crying old man—filthy bandages barely hanging onto his bleeding, crawling wounds. You stand there and stare at your feet because you just can't bear to look, and you know you will never be the same.

11 THE HOLY FAMILY

here was this one day . . . It's a day that took me years to even consider writing about. It haunts me still. Miriam and I were walking down the main drag in Calcutta when we came upon a couple sitting on the sidewalk. The woman was holding a baby who could not have been more than a week or two old. I will never forget the look in that mother's eyes. It was such a pleading, desperate, sad look. We kneeled down at their level to see the baby. I remember smiling at the woman, looking at the infant, and saying how beautiful she was. We didn't speak her language, but I tried to convey some kindness through my face and my tone of voice.

I laid a hand on the baby's head as if to give a blessing. I didn't know what else to do. Then we lingered a little before moving on. It was a touching and profoundly sad encounter. I wished I could have taken them home, cared for them, adopted the baby, something! Later, as I looked back on the experience, it dawned on me that I could have—should have—given them some money. What was I thinking? I think that I was already pretty fed up with the constant barrage of demands for money from people on the street. Everywhere we went, people were at us with their hands out and I became cold to it. So, when I came upon this desperate couple, I guess I somehow flicked a switch and took a stand. *No more!* I said inside. *I'm not made of money! Who do they think I am? A rich celebrity who can help everyone? Well I'm not and I can't.* I hardened my heart to the people whose need for charity may have been a matter of life or death. That baby didn't look too healthy or well fed.

Looking back, I wonder, did the mother give birth outside on the street? Did she have any help at all? Did she suffer needlessly? The memory of this experience has bothered me more as time has gone on. Four years later, I gave birth to my first child back home in Canada. She was a perfectly healthy, beautiful baby girl. I had had two baby showers and we were given everything we could possibly need to make baby's first year great, and a whole host of social supports too. Family and friends waited for long hours in the hospital as I labored, praying, and anxiously awaiting the little one's arrival. People came in steady streams to see us in the hospital, with more gifts and tokens of love. It was lovely, but again, not unexpected. Once home, we had people bringing food and offering to help with Catherine while mom and dad rested from the marathon of the past few days. I had everything I could possibly need and much more. All was well. All, except for the memories I was having about that lovely, dark-skinned couple with the tiny baby whom I met on the street in Calcutta. Where were they now? I wondered. I could not help wondering if they had had even a small fraction of the support that we had enjoyed. Did they even have their daily bread? Any friends to talk to and to hold the baby when they needed rest? Did they have anywhere to rest? Did the baby even live?

That dear little family on the street had, I assumed, not much more than the clothes on their backs. I could not help continuously asking myself, where is the justice, the fairness, the compassion? How can I have so much, and she have so little? Are we so different? What if I had been born there, and found myself having my baby in abject poverty? And what if I had complications there? Would I have had access to a hospital, to the medical intervention that was required to help deliver Catherine? And if not, would she have survived? Would I? I had a hard time bouncing back from the delivery, having lost a lot of blood. What shape would I have been in without all that help?

In my imagination, I dream that a lovely, benevolent person came upon that little family on the street not long after we walked away. Some generous stranger felt deep compassion and was moved to action, pressing many hundreds of rupees into the mother's hand and taking the father aside to offer him a job. Then the Good Samaritan took them into his very own home and tucked the three of them under his wing. They were nourished, looked after, and medically treated until they were ready to go out and find their own place to rest their heads—a place to call home. In my waking dream, the baby grows into an energetic child full of ideas, enthusiasm, and giggles. Mom stays home in their small but adequate house and takes in tailoring work while dad works at a satisfying job at a local newspaper. It turns out well after all. All they needed was a break.

I ask God to bless them whenever they cross my mind and I am sure that he does. Those dear little ones, so vulnerable, so poor. How could God help but take care of them? At the end of the day, I have to trust that he did and does care for them, and has not forgotten them. My task now is to forgive myself, to free myself from the endless mental loop of guilt, remorse, shame, and profound regret. I can't go back and find them and be the one who presses those rupees into their hands. But I can be tuned into the needs of those in need around me each day, here and now, and choose not to walk away. May I be worthy.

12 RUNNING ON EMPTIES

One day, Miriam and I were exploring Calcutta and doing a little sightseeing on foot. We toured the Victoria Memorial and then walked the expansive grounds, which are now a very busy park. We sat a while in the shade of a huge fountain, a few moments of relief from the scorching midday heat.

The park was bustling. Couples were strolling, young people were sunbathing, and families were picnicking and playing ball. It crossed my mind that I could really go for a cold Coke. Miriam concurred. We hopped up, found a little refreshment stand and each bought one. The tall, old-fashioned glass bottles the vendor gave us were a nice novelty; back home they'd long since switched over to plastic bottles. The man popped the caps off with a bottle opener, which was attached to his cart with a rope, and we were on our way. I took several big glugs of the stuff, bracing for the rush of pins and needles in my throat. It was worth it.

We walked along, chatting about this or that, meandering and taking photos of each other. And we both tried, unsuccessfully, to suppress guttural Coke burps—the kind that bring instant relief while momentarily stinging your nose. Then it was on; bent on out-burping each other, we laughed our heads off as we walked. I guess because we were laughing and goofing around, we didn't notice it right away but soon enough, it had our attention: someone was hollering behind us.

We stopped and turned to check out the commotion. It was the man who had sold us the Cokes, lumbering toward us, his arms flailing. We didn't need to speak the language to see that he was mad. Miriam and I glanced at each other quizzically. We'd paid for them. So what was his problem? Figuring he must be after someone else, we picked up the pace, anxious to get out of his warpath. This only made him madder and he made a beeline for us, still yelling. Miriam suddenly stopped, wheeled around, and looked him in the eye. The man stopped short, a little taken aback, but no less annoyed. "What's your problem?" she demanded, "why are you following us?" I'd never seen her cross like this. She meant business. The man pointed at the glass Coke bottles, reaching for them. He wanted them back. I was incensed! But Miriam softened, saying, "Ohhh! Okay. Sorry!" She put up an index finger, to tell him to wait a moment, while we finished drinking our Cokes. The man, now a little less upset, glanced back toward his stand. He needed to get back to it. We drained our Cokes and handed the bottles back to the man. He grabbed them and took off, glancing back at us, shaking his head and muttering to himself.

I turned to Miriam: "Can you believe that guy?" and I was off and running. "He screamed at us! He had no business treating us like that. We are paying customers!" She shrugged and said that no harm was done. I couldn't believe it. Of course, harm was done! I wasn't going to let it go without working up a good head of steam. "It's the principle of the thing," I said. "You can't go around harassing unsuspecting tourists like that. I've got a good mind to . . ." And then, it happened. In spite of myself, I let out a massive burp, the kind that makes your eyes water. Miriam laughed loudly and then she burped herself. My bad mood vanished and we started one of our crazy laughing attacks, stumbling along as though we'd just chugged more than just Coca Cola.

After all that, I felt so refreshed, so recharged, and ready to face whatever might come next. Miriam reached her arm around my shoulder and gave me a squeeze and said, "See, everything turned out okay." She was right. Again. I had this feeling God was teaching me some important lessons: That things aren't usually as bad as I think. That I could let go and trust him. And that people are mostly good and kind, just as long as you don't steal their bottles.

13 I'M JUST ONE PERSON

One afternoon in Calcutta, I walked out of the money exchange store and started heading up the street. I turned and noticed some people begging across the way. They were watching me. I had just cashed some more of my travelers' checks so I could pay my hotel bill.

I turned a corner and stopped into a small grocery store. Suddenly I felt very guilty and wondered why I had so much and many of these people had little or nothing. Father John had told me that I could live in India quite comfortably for six months with the money I had brought for six weeks: $600. It occurred to me that I could do a lot of good with that money.

My mind reeled with the possibilities. I could cash in my RRSPs (a Canadian retirement savings plan), do odd jobs at home for a while, and then come back, get a big place, and take in as many people as I could. Think of the potential for ministry, rehabilitation, retraining! Maybe I'd even teach English and sewing and who knows what else. Yes, that was it! I would go home, drum up some major fundraising dollars from all the churches, then go back and, who knows? Suddenly, I was Oscar

Schindler, desperate to come up with ways to save more and more of them. How else could I have survived there if I didn't somehow start piecing together a viable plan to help these destitute people? This is a crisis! Doesn't anybody see? I wanted to run home and shout from the rooftops: "People are sleeping and living on the filthy streets in Calcutta! Bombay! Bangalore! What are we waiting for? This is an epidemic! Somebody help me!" This was my great plan of salvation taking shape. Surely it was doable, wasn't it? I could make a difference, relieve their suffering, help them turn things around, right? Right? How could I stand by and do nothing?

The days passed and reality started falling heavily on me. I wasn't going to be turning things around for the poor in Calcutta. Systemic change would ultimately need to happen to relieve their suffering. The world already has a Savior, and it's not me. So, as is my tendency, I swung over to the other extreme. Clearly there was nothing I could do. This problem, this tragedy, this condition, was bigger than me and my churches back home. How could I possibly have thought that I, Stephanie Emmons, 27-year-old do-gooder from North America, could possibly do anything to relieve suffering on a scale as grand as this? On any scale? I could not.

I let myself fall into some kind of a depression, or at least a pretty good funk. Why did I even bother to come here? I spent $1200 of my own money on the flight alone, and for what? To come and be a voyeur, looking at people's pain and suffering, which I was powerless to do a damn thing about. They weren't tourist attractions, for heaven's sake, these children in the orphanage. We foreigners, or better yet, tourists, would parade around the cribs and tour the rooms looking at all the poor little orphans. At least—I told myself—at least maybe some of them are here to choose a child to adopt, in which case this viewing would make sense. But no. I was told that Indian children couldn't be adopted outside the country. I felt sick. Why were they there? Why was I there? What was it that drew us to come and look at these babies no one wanted? No one besides Mother Teresa. I felt ashamed.

Then I remembered Mother Teresa's words to us when we had first met: "Go spend time with the children." She had made a point of telling us to go to them. Of course. Mother Teresa knew that we weren't self-seeking tourists, hanging about in India for nothing better than to get a good story to tell back home. She looked into our faces and I think she knew. We were there because of our love for God. We were answering a deeply personal call. What else could have motivated us to disrupt our lives, spend our money, and travel to a foreign place so far from the comforts of home? Mother Teresa knew that we would not make a dent in the poverty situation in Calcutta. She didn't commission us to "Go forth and build great centers of rehabilitation and salvation and ministry." She didn't ask us to donate money to her cause. She didn't even ask how long we could stay. She just asked us to be present, to spend time with them.

As it happened, a week later, while on the train heading back to Cochin, I was reading *A Simple Path* by Lucinda Vardey. (A great book; I recommend it to you.) Lucinda had spent time with Mother Teresa and wrote the book about her ministry and her spiritual path. In her book, I came across the following story of a man who was reflecting on an experience he had once had when volunteering with the Missionaries of Charity. In his words: "I hadn't done much. I mostly sat on people's beds and stroked them or fed them. . . . When the sister asked how I'd got on, I said, 'I was there.' And she said to me, 'what was St. John or Our Blessed Mother doing at the foot of the cross?' "

14 HAPPINESS IS A FRESH TURKEY SANDWICH

After several weeks of eating mostly rice, chickpeas, chapattis, and some bananas, I started to have the craziest craving for a turkey sandwich. Here's how the fantasy went: thick, soft white crusty bread with mayo, piled high with freshly shaved oven roasted turkey, with a sour dill pickle on the side. Pair it up with a tall glass of cold milk, and there you have it: heaven on a plate.

Deli meats and crusty white North American-type bakery bread were in short supply where we were, and as I daydreamed about my sandwich it began to take on unusual proportions and qualities. I could see it on a pedestal in my mind. I could smell the fresh-baked bread, see the turkey peeking out the side, and I could almost taste the savory meat slathered with the creamy full-fat mayo. The image of my sandwich became the object of my habitual daydreams, my mini-vacation from the reality of Calcutta.

One day, when we awoke to the beep-beep-beep of our travel alarm at 5:00 a.m. as usual, I knew I could not leave the room. I would not be joining Miriam on our daily half-hour excursion through the streets of Calcutta toward the Mother House of the Missionaries of Charity. Mass was celebrated there daily at 6 a.m., and we hadn't missed one since arriving a week earlier. But on this day, my body, mind, and soul sent up a non-negotiable "NO." Miriam encouraged me to push myself to get up and go, but I just couldn't. So off she went on her own, after being reassured that I would be fine.

We had recently made friends with a group from YWAM: Youth with a Mission that had just arrived at the guesthouse. They were from Southern Ontario—just a few hours' drive from where we lived in Canada. They were thrilled to have Miriam as their guide, to help them reach the Mother House, and show them the ropes. So, off they went, too.

Alone at last, I lay back on my bed and studied the cracks in the grey ceiling. Except for a couple of bathroom trips, I didn't move from that spot until late in the afternoon. Something had deeply disturbed me over the previous few days and I needed to just stay there quietly, unmoving for a while. I felt I would never be the same again. Something had broken. I couldn't cry; I just lay there feeling nauseous, shaky, and so very tired.

What was it that had shaken me so? Maybe I had been unsettled by the two aggressive adolescent boys who accosted us on the street yelling "Sister! Sister!" They grabbed us, pulling us forcefully, motioning us to go with them. Miriam and I, both resisting, shot a worried glance at each other as it happened. It was abrupt and startling, and the boys seemed adamant and determined. They each had one of us, grasping both wrists, and were bodily pulling us with them against our will. "NO!" I yelled, pulling back with all my strength. But they persisted, and I realized that this boy was stronger than me. He overpowered me. "Sister!" They continued to yell, dragging us along. Finally, they had let go, and brought us to a large outdoor candy stand. They pointed enthusiastically to the sweets, still yelling.

I was so freaked out by the way they had dragged me along that I just turned away and took off, Miriam right on my heels. Fortunately, the boys didn't pursue us. That experience had really shaken us up, and we were both jumpy for the rest of the day.

I replayed all of this in my mind as I lay there, in and out of sleep in the big bedroom. Then I recalled the people and villages we had passed in the train as we had traveled across India to get here. What stood out to me was their simple tattered dress, their meager deteriorating huts, the looks of resignation, and the sense of emptiness on their faces. They stood along the railroad tracks, just behind the barrier. It seemed they were looking longingly at the train as it ambled along. Were they wishing it would stop and take them away somewhere? Were they hoping someone would open a window and throw them some money or something to eat? Did they know I was on the other side of the glass with my $600—enough to sustain their whole family for months? Every village looked the same.

I thought of the small boy who came on the train at one of the long stops. He was filthy and barely dressed. Standing right in front of us, he was pleading with his eyes. I thought of the legions of other children who called Calcutta's Howrah Train Station their home. Their home! It had been easy enough to give a few rupees to the boy on the train. But what to do with the rest of them? The hundreds and hundreds of other destitute people, trying to survive another day. How on earth could I help them all? How could I not? All of their faces were before me as I lay there on the bed and I just couldn't think anymore.

It was then that some kind of protective shield started to come over me. I'd heard that the brain protects us from trauma when it's had too much. Witnessing that level of raw suffering, need, and desperation, over and over, and being helpless to do anything about it—it did something to me. It made me need to stare at the ceiling for hours on end, trying to make sense of the senseless. It made me feel guilty for having been born in a place where there is an abundance of clean water, food, shelter, and so much more. It made me go around and give away almost all of the clothes in my suitcase. But I had to find a balance and put a cap on it somewhere. Otherwise, a couple of naïve-looking foreigners like us didn't stand a chance against the many pairs of sad eyes at every turn. But we wanted to help each one.

How could we refuse people who clearly had needs beyond our comprehension—beyond anything we had ever seen back home? There was no choice; it was simply a case of self-preservation. If we indulged every request we received, we would soon be unable to take care of our own needs. It felt like a real lose-lose situation, and a feeling of something like despair started creeping in.

Of course, Calcutta was unlike any place I had ever been. And I think a big part of why I needed to rest and be alone was the noise—the constant clamor of the vehicles, coming and going, the honking, the cries, the street music. I hadn't anticipated the many types of loud music blasting everywhere. It seemed like every shop was bent on outdoing the others in volume, creating a rising cacophony of indistinguishable songs. Add all of this to the loud blare of some of the street celebrations (I can't remember which Hindu god or gods' birthday they were celebrating that week) combined to make one resounding, continuous noise. And the celebrations often continued day and night for days. At least at night, the volume went down, a little bit.

The glassless, shutterless windows where we stayed had only screens, so there was no way to shut out the noise. No escape. I discovered the bliss of earplugs during that trip, though they could only do so much. So, as I lay there, trying to shut out the noise, both outside the building and inside my head, I found myself latching on to the familiar image of my lovely turkey sandwich. It became my mind's benevolent diversion. Whenever my thoughts raced and my feelings threatened to overwhelm, I summoned the comforting vision of my sandwich. It grounded me, reminding me of home. It reminded me that, soon enough, I would be back on Canadian soil. Forty days, I thought.

How could I have brought myself here to India for forty days? Months of planning for it, years of dreaming about it, and here I was, three weeks in, terrified and desperate. Desperate to get back home. Sometimes, I could think of little else.

Meanwhile, Miriam was having the time of her life. She jumped into every new situation with both feet. She didn't seem to understand my fear, my agitation, my hyper-vigilance, and I couldn't expect her to. I didn't get it either. In her casual, carefree way, she would lovingly admonish me to just get past it and enjoy being in India. I really wanted to do that, but I could not. I knew that my worries and increasing fragility were not conducive to Miriam's enjoyment of India, but I felt unable to do, or be, otherwise. And while her lightheartedness was comforting and endearing, sometimes I felt utterly alone.

Communicating with home was not easy. I soon came to feel that we are ultimately alone in this world, except for the Lord. I know that God was lovingly using my distress and loneliness to show me that at the end of the day, it's really only him and me and that that should be enough. And as I would soon discover, his presence isn't just enough—it's everything.

15 HAVING NOTHING, AND YET POSSESSING EVERYTHING

When I think about why I went there, I have to admit that I wanted to see if something of the Missionaries of Charity might rub off on me. I hoped that maybe, just by being there, hanging around the Sisters, going to daily Mass at 6 a.m.—brutal for a night owl like me—and being eager to volunteer, maybe somehow I would get a glimpse into the mystery. I mean, who does that? How can they live like that? It still blows my mind that I actually went.

I had always wanted to meet Mother Teresa, and she wasn't getting any younger. And I'd always wanted to see and experience firsthand what it was that she called the poorest of the poor. But there was something more. I think that the reason I really went—besides all the noble ones—was to see if she was for real. I needed to look into those sisters' faces and see if they were for real, if what you see is what you get. They owned nothing—just a couple of saris, a pair of sandals, a few personal items, a sweater, and a Bible. I think that's pretty much the extent of the possessions that the Missionaries of Charity have to their names. I wondered how they could they find fulfillment in living a life like that. No trips to the beach, no dinners and movies and coffee with friends, no TV, no nothing. The thought of it unnerved me—still unnerves me. Admitting this is humbling.

But there it was: joy. Everywhere. I saw joy on the faces of the sisters as they washed their saris in tin buckets. Joy as they processed into the huge, sparse chapel to celebrate Mass or pray the Rosary. And again—joy as they saw us volunteers off for the day's work in one of their homes. Joy! Where was it coming from? Why did they look so happy having nothing? They would not be raising their own family, writing a book, traveling the world, accomplishing great things! These were the things I had wanted, or thought I wanted. But I did not feel joy. So there you have it. The real reason I went to see Mother Teresa and the Missionaries of Charity in action was to go and see what they had that I didn't have, knew that I didn't know, saw that I didn't see. And what I saw, well . . . they had so much. They had community. They were a family. They had clarity of purpose. They knew what they were supposed to be doing with their lives and they were doing it. They had structure, a roof over their heads, food to eat, and daily prayer time together. And they had Jesus. Or should I say, Jesus had them. He had, at some point in each of their lives, whispered an invitation to walk with him, to be his hands and feet in the world, to serve him in the person of the poor. They were to be Christ among the world, and it brought them such joy.

It was clear that these women were not living an austere life of emptiness at all—at least, not in the way I had thought. It was a life of fullness. This was hard for my materialistic brain to grasp back then. In my twenties I'd often wondered whether God was calling me to join a faith community, to become a part of a purposeful whole, but what about my life? My family? My friends? My hopes and dreams? All my *stuff*? *How*, I would often ask myself, *did they reconcile a deep desire to follow God with an attachment to the things of the world?* Seemed to me something of a superhuman feat. Now, as I cast my memory back to reflect on this question again, I'm not sure I am any closer to an answer, although the desire to find one is just as strong. Resisting the urge to check my iPhone for the tenth time in the last hour, I'll humbly admit that this is a much broader question than when I first wrote it in my journal all those years ago.

16 LEAVING MOTHER TERESA

A s our last day in Calcutta drew closer, little waves of sadness came and went. I felt fragile as the sting of losing my Grandma visited me, no doubt stirred up by the impending farewell to another beloved mother figure. We hadn't known Mother Teresa for long—just a few short weeks—but that didn't matter. She had captured our hearts.

And then it was upon us: February 2—departure day. A few short weeks earlier, I had longed for this day, but so much had happened and now everything was different. I was different. And I didn't want to face the thought of leaving her.

We attended 6 a.m. Mass at the Motherhouse for the last time that morning. During the few minutes of silent prayer, after the priest had distributed the Eucharist, it occurred to me that we would never see Mother again. It was almost time to say goodbye. I felt oddly unbalanced, suddenly very tired.

When Mass was concluded, Miriam and I went to see Mother in the hallway outside the chapel chatting with some other volunteers. Soon they were off, and she turned her attention toward us. We told her we were on our way to Howrah Station to take the train back to Cochin. I had wanted to tell her how much I loved meeting her and working with the sisters and other volunteers, how incredibly special it had all been, how I would never forget her . . . but those words didn't really come. Instead, we just made a bit of small talk. I forget the particulars of the conversation, but one thing was clear—we were visibly sad.

She smiled at us warmly, holding Miriam's hands as we chatted, and then mine, looking up in our faces, in turn. Mother gave each of us a small oval medal with the image of Jesus on it. And then, with a playful flourish and wry grin, she said, "My card," handing each of us a little yellow card. A Hindu businessman had kindly had one of her prayers printed on "business cards" for her:

The fruit of SILENCE is Prayer
The fruit of PRAYER is Faith
The fruit of FAITH is Love
The fruit of LOVE is Service
The fruit of SERVICE is Peace

Mother Teresa

She joked around a bit more with us and then, slowly, in her very thick accent, she said, "I am praying that when I see you again, you're wearing one of these," pointing to her sari. I laughed nervously and I said something terribly clever like, "You never know, Mother!" She laughed. We laughed.

So the last memories we have of Mother Teresa are of a woman who chuckled and joked around just as easily as anyone else I knew. She was so normal. There she was, standing there cheering us up, as though she had nowhere else to be. This was a woman who had known sadness and pain. But in *our* difficult moment, she made us laugh. She had been known to tell her sisters to "Never let anyone come to you without coming away better and happier." Mission accomplished.

17 A VALENTINE'S HOMECOMING

returned home to Ottawa after forty days away. I had heard about something called reverse culture shock but had never given it much thought. Raised by a loving family in a peaceful, first-world country, I had never known hardship. And until that Valentine's Day in 1996, I had no idea just how sweet it was to live in Canada.

I made my way off the crowded plane, regretting having chosen a seat way in the back. As I walked through the tunnel connecting the plane to the airport, my heart raced and my mind reeled. Am I really here? Really home? I wondered who would be at the airport to greet me. Dad had said he would come if he could. Rounding the corner into the arrivals area, I saw happy reunions and homecomings all around; it was a flurry of hearts and flowers. Then I saw them across the room in those familiar hands: pink carnations. My Dad was holding them, smiling. I could see the relief, joy, and love on his face. He had come for me and was going to take me home. My brother Rob was there too. I started to cry.

It had been a hard few weeks, and it occurred to me that this couldn't have been an easy time for my family either. The love and anticipation on their faces touched me deeply as I crossed the large room. I rushed over to them and pretty much fell into my father's arms. I was safe. I was 26 years old and hadn't lived at home in several years. Still, I happily accepted that familiar parental comfort. *I'm so glad Dad's come*, I thought. *He's come for me.* After six, long, unraveling weeks during which home sometimes felt very far away, my Dad had come for me. I think that that day in the airport, God was present in the person of my father, showing me that I was never alone. What better way to experience the abundant care of God than through the strong, loving embrace of my own Dad.

Rob and Dad picked up my bag at the luggage carousel, carried it to the car, and took me home. The little place I had left six weeks earlier was a simple two-bedroom apartment I shared with my friend Sarah. I'd often grumbled that it was too small, too old, and the tiny galley kitchen had barely enough counter space. The place was adequate with nothing to spare. But on my return, something really weird happened. The place appeared vast—and so clean. Even the formerly crappy little kitchen seemed bigger, nicer, and almost modern. I slowly walked around my apartment, looking at everything we had. It was so strange. Was this really my place? I felt a bit light-headed, and a dull ache in the back of my head was making its way toward my temples.

My body felt heavy. I thought I might be sick. Rob got me to sit on the couch and put my feet up on the coffee table. Dad encouraged me to rest. "I'm sure you're exhausted. You'll feel better after you sleep," he said. He was right: I slept almost twelve hours that night. It took a while before I stopped feeling disoriented and just plain lousy.

Thankfully, my friend and boss, Susan, had encouraged me to take a couple extra days off when I got home. Susan founded Ottawa Innercity Ministries in 1988, and at the time of the trip I worked for OIM as coordinator of volunteers and street outreach. Susan knew from experience that I would need time to readjust to so many things, like extreme jetlag, the cold weather, and my life in general.

My life . . . How was I going to go back to that? Leading up to the trip, I'd worked so hard to prepare for every eventuality, both in India, and while in transit. But I wasn't ready for what would happen to me in the days and weeks that followed my coming home. I was blindsided. Waves of strong feelings hit me at random times: sadness, anxiety, the odd bit of euphoria. . . . But it was the anger that really came out of left field. I tried to talk myself out of it, saying unhelpful things like, "Come on. You have had the trip of a lifetime. What's there to be angry about? You've got memories and photos, stories to tell your grandkids about. Why the sadness?"

I told myself to be grateful. I mean—I had met Mother Teresa! Seriously. Who gets to do that? The way I saw it, I had no right to complain or entertain self-pity. And yet, everything seemed to annoy me or make me tear up. I had little patience for trivial things. Even months later, whenever someone asked to see the pictures or hear about the trip, I would take a deep breath and just get through it. I was so torn; I really did want to share everything, but I still felt so raw.

One day I just knew I had to draw a hard line between India and me. I had to get it all out of my sight: my photo albums, my souvenirs, my letters from Uncle Frank—all of it. So I spread everything out on my bed and took one last look. Then I gathered everything together and placed it in a big white plastic bag—the one from the store where Miriam and I had bought our saris in Cochin. Folding it over nice and tight, I ceremoniously placed the bundle in a cardboard banker's box and hoisted it onto a high shelf in my bedroom closet. I was quite pleased with myself, confident that my little time capsule would afford me some peace. I would, however, learn that that's not how it works with trauma, grief, or whatever this horror was.

I couldn't shake the images in my mind or the feelings that still dogged me. The smell of burning wood or tires brought me right back there. Loud, sudden noises made me jump. It slowly dawned on me that I was no longer the same person who had boarded a plane not so long before. Not really. When you meet people whose whole lives are spent begging on the street— some with no legs, others with no arms, still others with no eyes or hands or feet or whatever, you are changed. When you've been hounded at a busy train station by an onslaught of filthy, desperate young children, you are changed. And when it hits you that some of the people you have so recently met have probably died by now, you're forever changed. But here I was:

home—safe and sound, flooded with a grief I could not name.
I would have to find a way to live with and let go of all the faces
I could still see, while not allowing myself to totally forget. As
if I ever could.

18 UNBELIEVABLE

ong before meeting Mother Teresa, I had heard about her sense of humor on more than one occasion. Apparently, she appreciated a good joke and liked to have fun, which I've always thought was cool. When I did eventually meet and talk with her, I got to experience this for myself. She was warm and friendly, and I remember that she was easy to talk to. There was just something about her—a depth and a kind of knowing look to her. She smiled at me the way my Grandma used to. With all the love in the world, with kind eyes that seemed to say, *I'm here, I see you, you matter,* but still casual somehow. Other heroes of mine, like the beloved Trappist monk Thomas Merton, are known to have had this same quality. I think that human warmth is a characteristic shared by many of the saints.

She did have a way of making people laugh. It stayed with me, that witty and unexpected side of her that she let us see. That's a memory of her that I've treasured since the first time we met. As my book took shape over the years, I've looked forward to telling readers about this, to offer a glimpse into this special and unique thing I'd experienced. It was a no-brainer.

Of course, I would tell about her kindness, her easy joyfulness, and the individual attention she paid to Miriam and me. But this other thing, this part where she was just playful for no reason except for the simple fun of it, well, that was another thing altogether. And while I knew that this was a precious pearl others would treasure too, it had never occurred to me to make of it the focus of the book, much less allude to it right there in the title. But that was before.

That was years before I would learn about a whole other side to Mother Teresa's life that no one could have guessed, even those closest to her. As it turns out, throughout her ministry to the poor—an astonishing fifty years—much of Mother Teresa's life was spent in what she called "the darkness." We know this because of the many letters she wrote about it to a handful of spiritual directors over the years, some of which, thankfully, they kept. In 2007, some of those letters were published in a book called *Come Be My Light*, edited by Father Brian Kolodiejchuk, of the Missionaries of Charity. As the book tells it, Mother Teresa had lost all sense of God's presence, love, and at times, his very existence. For so long, she had suffered what has been referred to as deep and abiding spiritual pain. (Mother Teresa! The Living Saint! I *know*!)

"[T]here is in my heart," she wrote, "a very deep union with the will of God. I accept not in my feelings but in my will."

I was flabbergasted. Besides initially feeling very bad for her, one of my first reactions was, *Are you kidding me?! If this* saint *isn't immune to spiritual bewilderment, what hope do I have?* I read the letters over and over, trying to grasp this jarring news, at first quite unable to absorb it. I just couldn't understand, let alone accept it. I looked online for a blog or forum—some discussion or something that might help me put words to what I was going through. I really needed to talk about it with someone! I felt unbalanced as I grappled with what it meant in terms of faith in God and so on. I could find no such community or discussion back then, so I feverishly filled pages and pages in my journal as I tried to figure it all out, as if figuring it out was even going to be possible.

The crazy thing is, my struggle would not have been nearly as difficult had I done more than just read the letters in the book. If I had taken a breath and stopped long enough to also read some of the editor's commentary, I think I would have had at least some measure of understanding, some means of coming to terms with Mother Teresa's experience. But that's not the way it unfolded. I would carry this around for several years before it occurred to me to pick up the book again. When I eventually did crack it and give it another go, this is what I read: "Interior darkness is nothing new in the tradition of Catholic mysticism. In fact, it has been a common phenomenon among the numerous saints throughout Church history who have experienced what the Spanish Carmelite mystic St. John of the Cross termed the 'dark night.' The spiritual master aptly employed this term to designate the painful purifications one undergoes before reaching union with God."

I wrestled with this. The thing is, I had met her all those years ago. That was not a woman in pain—not the kind the book was describing . . . at least, not that *I* could see. Yet I did believe she penned those letters. The person who had compiled and published them in the book was her friend, a priest, and a member of the Missionaries of Charity himself. He had no reason to make this up. I thought back to our little interactions, trying to carefully sift through every moment, every possible nuanced memory I had of her, no matter how small. But I didn't sense even a whiff of what her letters described. (And yes I'm aware of how this sounds now—that I, a random, twenty-something volunteer from the other side of the world, having met her just a handful of times more than ten years earlier, would be in a position to detect and discern what was deep in her heart—that which she had hidden from her closest friends. Yeah. I'm humbled as I tell this part to you, but there it is.)

As you can imagine, being in the saint's presence was pure bliss. Who wouldn't want to goof around with Mother Teresa? I will always treasure those blessed, rare moments. But considered in light of her distress, a deeper story unfolds. And though some have suggested that by hiding it Mother Teresa was dishonest or uncharitable, it's not quite that simple. In fact, keeping it to herself may have been one of her greatest acts of charity, and that's saying something.

Mother Teresa belonged to the world. In a sense, she was everyone's mother. She was certainly mother to her thousands of Missionaries of Charity across the globe. As Father Brian said in the book, "She was a guide, a teacher, an example, but in all she was always a mother." With this in mind, what mother would burden her children with the knowledge that she was hurting, to the extent that she was? What mother tells her child that she feels God has abandoned her? To what end? At what cost? It's absurd. I can imagine that Mother Teresa carefully considered what there could possibly be to gain, only coming up empty. She knew. Disclosure to anyone beyond absolute necessity ran the risk of causing great harm. No matter how much she may have wanted to come clean and let someone in, there was no way. To do so would have been reckless. Imagine the headlines: "*God Abandons Mother Teresa!*" To have admitted to her flock that she had lost sight of God and struggled to make sense of his absence would have flown in the face of everything that had made her a good mother and spiritual leader in the first place. No, her journey was to be a solitary one. Like her patron saint St. Therese of Lisieux during her own trial of faith in the last eighteen months of her life, Mother Teresa feared that her thoughts were blasphemous. . . . She feared that her words might be a cause of scandal or temptation to others.

She did not want the truth of her spiritual struggle to ever be revealed. She was deeply concerned that if it became known, it might lead people to believe that God is not to be trusted or even believed in at all. It's a fair point, but consider this: Mother Teresa, a self-described worthless little follower of Jesus who could do nothing without God, felt abandoned and deeply anguished for much of her ministry and yet she kept going, day after day, year after year, for almost fifty years.

"If you only knew what goes on within my heart. Sometimes the pain is so great that I feel as if everything will break. The smile is a big cloak, which covers a multitude of pains," she said. How it saddens me all over again to read those words.

The thing is, when we met her, not only did she *not* show her anguish—she made us laugh. Somehow, she pushed past her pain, stepped beyond herself, and reached out to connect. Whatever God's reasoning behind Mother Teresa's dark night of the soul, it would not be open to scrutiny in the court of public opinion in those days. No one would be the wiser. Father Michael van der Peet, a friend, once expressed it this way: "Whenever I met Mother, all self-consciousness left me. I felt right away at ease: she radiated peace and joy, even when she shared with me the darkness in her spiritual life. I was often amazed that someone who lived so much face to face with suffering people and went through the dark night herself, still could make you feel happy. . . ." Actually this does make sense to me. She took her Lord Jesus literally when he said that whatever we do to the least among us, we do to him (Matthew 25:35). And, as her whole life was all about Jesus, of course she wanted to please him and serve him, not only in the poor, but in each person she met, regardless of how she felt. She was the perfect hostess to the Perfect Guest she perceived in each of us. And though we now know what a burden this was, she clearly considered it a small price to pay against her ultimate goal— eternity in Paradise with the One she loved.

Mother Teresa was a human being. Clearly. But it helps to remind myself of that sometimes, especially now that we Catholics call her St. Teresa of Calcutta. It makes her seem less distant and ethereal to me, knowing she could relate to a lot of the hard stuff we go through, including sometimes struggling with our faith.

I mean, if *Saint* Mother Teresa wasn't immune to times of doubt and disillusionment about God, why should I be any different? I've read some of the things the scholars and theologians have to say about this concept of the dark night of the soul. I've tried to get my head around the wisdom of ancient mystics like St. John of the Cross and St. Teresa of Avila who seem to have known a lot about these things. And while it's mysterious and intriguing and everything, I also find it troubling.

I am a cradle Catholic, meaning that I have been a Roman Catholic from the time I was baptized as an infant. And while I don't remember or profess to have retained everything I was taught about the faith during my school years at Pope John XXIII and St. Pius X schools, I do have a decent enough grasp of it all. Nevertheless, I confess I am stumped. It's beyond me. For years I have racked my brains trying to figure out this dark night stuff. How can I raise all of the disconcerting questions I raise in this book, reflecting on the reason for suffering itself, without understanding what many theologians and spiritual writers describe as this other kind of suffering—suffered by the Mother Teresa who made me laugh—in the dark night of the soul?

I recently came across an angle to understanding that I really like. Rabbi Harold Kushner, in his beautiful and massively popular book *When Bad Things Happen to Good People,* approaches it this way: The word "answer" can mean "response" as well as "explanation." The answers we go around looking for, or begging God to give to us in ways we understand, may not come with "explanations." Kushner suggests that the more important question is not why the bad things happen, but how we will respond to them. He says that God's role in human suffering is "to stand with us, giving us courage and strength and empowering us to respond with compassion and forgiveness." So maybe it's not so much about finding some satisfying answers and wrapping them all up in a tidy package so we have something tangible to point to. It might be more a case of living the unanswered questions, drawing closer to God and trusting he will reveal things in his time.

19 IF THERE BE GOD

t is one thing for a person to wonder what God is doing or if he's even doing anything at all. But it's something else altogether to question his existence, to utter words like these: "If there be God, please forgive me." And it's especially astonishing that a saint—a real, bona fide, canonized saint, such as Mother Teresa—might have said these words. Yet this is part of a prayer she wrote and included in a letter to her bishop, in whom she had confided. She not only wrestled with her sense of God's absence, but at times, even his very existence. Even then, her strong faith is manifested immediately in the part of the phrase where she asks for forgiveness. It seems as if she's saying to God, *I feel like you might not exist, but of course I know you do, therefore please forgive me for even entertaining this.*

The thing is, day after day, year after year, Mother Teresa walked the walk. Loving, serving, persevering, and running a worldwide organization—all the while feeling no consolation from the One who had called her to this work in the first place. No revelations. Nothing. But she didn't want anyone to know, in case it might cause some to doubt the Lord or question her devotion to the poor. She tried to make sense of it, aching in vain for a sign, just a word or a touch. And though none came, she got up every morning, put on her worn white sari with the blue stripe, pinned the crucifix on her shoulder, slipped her tired feet into very tired secondhand sandals that had no business on the feet of a saint, and she carried on.

The fact that she had little spiritual consolation didn't stop her from loving and opening up to others. It didn't prevent her from putting one foot in front of the other every day. And she was not just serving the poor, but managing a worldwide ministry, including all the travel, diplomacy, red tape, courage, and perseverance that was required of her. She suffered a lot. Thankfully, she also managed to laugh a lot. And she was instrumental in helping countless thousands worldwide. Well, if that isn't a testament of the power of the God she served, I can't think of what it would be.

But still . . . I cannot imagine what that does to a person. Sure, she was Mother Teresa, but she was human. Where was Jesus? What about the presence of the One with whom she had so often walked and talked—her Beloved? That emptiness— the "darkness" as she called it—that felt absence of God, the total lack of anything resembling the close companionship they had so recently enjoyed—where was this? What was this? Decades passed and nothing changed. This breaks my heart— the knowledge that one so holy, so obedient perceived that she had lost God's favor.

Despite what some of the media or her critics called it, what Mother Teresa experienced wasn't a crisis or a lack of faith. Rather, it was a trial of faith where she experienced the feeling that she did not believe in God. So while she (and others) may have wondered whether she had lost her faith, that just wasn't the case. To illustrate this, Father Paul Murray, a close friend of Mother's for years, offers this explanation of the seemingly unexplainable: "This darkness was not . . . an experience of depression or despair. Rather it was the shadow cast in her soul by the overwhelming light of God's presence: God utterly present yet utterly hidden. His intimate, purifying love experienced as a devastating absence, and even on occasion, as a complete abandonment."

The God who made the plan for her to begin and sustain the Missionaries of Charity clearly had his own reasons for what was happening. That she didn't know why or even sometimes wondered whether God existed, but she still kept carrying out this plan—this tells me that God is real. Regardless of the painful feelings around it, her faith in this God was such that she was given the ability to carry on no matter what. Only God could enable a person to do what she did. Only God could be at the root of this. No human power could have accomplished any of this.

Just the same, I don't understand why she had to endure that endless dark night. I don't know why a loving God would have her go through that while expecting her to keep on, day after day. I don't understand. I really don't. But I believe that he is a loving God and I also believe that there is a plan, and the plan is good. And I bet if I could sit down with Mother Teresa today, she would say that all is well, and all is as it should be or something equally cryptic yet reassuring.

When I learned that she had suffered for most of the years of her ministry, feeling a marked absence of God's presence, I was floored. What legitimacy was there to her words if she was hiding the fact that she often felt abandoned by him? I felt betrayed. It was all so confusing. Hadn't she spoken so often about God's love and mercy? And what about the joy of loving and serving Jesus her beloved in the poorest of the poor? I walked around feeling out of sorts and preoccupied for a few weeks. I, and many others, just couldn't understand. Why had she behaved one way while feeling another? Where was the integrity in that? Why had she so often talked about sharing the joy of Christ with each person we meet, when she herself could barely recall what it meant to feel joy? Worst of all, in her darkest moments she occasionally doubted not only her calling but also her very belief in God. But she came off as peaceful! Radiant. Inspiring. Selfless. Saintly. Her critics threw around awful words like fraud and deception. I read that Mother Teresa had pleaded that her personal writings be destroyed, and I can see why; she feared this very thing.

And yet . . . what explanation did she owe me, or anyone else? What right had I to judge her? I can only imagine the universal outcry of betrayal had she been entirely forthright, admitting she didn't know for sure whether God had inspired her calling or that he was even with her at all. She knew the harm it would cause her community if she stood in front of them one day and announced that she felt tremendous despair. No, she was their leader. It was precisely her willingness to serve God by offering what she called wholehearted free service to the poorest of the poor that had called forth the same thing in them. She couldn't possibly have come clean about this—not to anyone.

But I still didn't understand. Why did it happen to her at all? This left me not only reeling from this knowledge of her struggle, but also with some huge questions: Why did God allow this? Why didn't God spare her this, or help her somehow? Why didn't he send her someone or something that could've brought her some relief or consolation? If God could let this be Mother Teresa's lot, who is to say it can't befall me or anyone else at any time? What kind of loving God does that? What could possibly have been gained by her suffering? Her loneliness? What was it all about? So it went, the endless mental loop. These unanswered questions just hung there in front of me, disturbing my sleep and blurring my days for a very long time. Few things in my life have disturbed me like this did. I wondered how I could ever hope to grow in faith and find a strong footing in God if Mother Teresa struggled to do so. I was taught that as Christians we are called to be saints—to follow a path that leads to holiness and closeness with God. But when all this other stuff was swirling around in my head, I really didn't know what to think.

But I kept coming back to this: she persevered. She kept going. It reminds me of St. Paul and his first-century companions. They endured many kinds of hardship—I mean, serious stuff like shipwrecks and beatings and imprisonment! Yet they kept going, even boldly proclaiming things like: "We do not lose heart" (2 Corinthians 4:16). But why not? Who does that? Weren't they only human? There's no way I would have been as steadfast in their place, so willing to hang in there no matter what. I know I would have been easily discouraged at all the opposition they encountered. I would have been terrified of the beatings, torture, and every kind of calamity that befell them. I'd have certainly cleared out at the first sign of trouble. I know it. But these followers of Jesus had these horrific things happen to them precisely because of him. Weren't they ever tempted to throw in the towel, to just walk away? At what point might it have become just too much? I seriously doubt I would have had the courage those early followers had.

When things started to get sketchy, Jesus asked Peter and his close circle whether they were planning to take off, like some of the other followers had. Peter's somewhat disquieting answer has echoed down through the centuries: "Lord, to whom shall we go" (John 6:68)? There was no alternative, no better path. They would go the distance with him. I imagine it must have been terribly daunting, knowing there was a real possibility of danger, maybe even death, the longer they hung out with this preacher. I can understand that they might well have considered going the way of those others who did turn away and move on. . . . But they didn't. They chose to stay. There must have been something so compelling about him in person, unlike any other figure that they had ever come across . . . a *something* that touched them and just reached them somehow. No matter the cost, no matter the pain and uncertainty, they knew that they had been called to be a part of something pretty great. It was worth it. *He* was worth it.

At the time of her calling in the early days, Mother Teresa knew she had been called to something unspeakably great, too. Her faithfulness to that call, no matter how she felt, and the example of perseverance she has given us is a gift that defies any words I can come up with. Fr. Paul Murray sums it up beautifully: "In particular, with regard to those among us who feel bewildered, at times, or even completely lost, but who are determined to keep walking along the path of faith, Teresa of Calcutta has become a source of enormous encouragement, a truly remarkable example of steadfastness and hope."

So I guess that, in the end, it's a comfort to know that, just like the rest of us, Mother Teresa experienced times of discouragement, despair, weariness of soul. In a word, Mother Teresa was human. And holy. She didn't have to be just one or the other. This makes her more accessible, and even relatable. I mean, if *the* Mother Teresa, literally the living saint of our times, could feel that kind of emptiness and yet still reach for a life of holiness, she shows us that it's possible.

I just came across a line in Thomas Merton's autobiography, *The Seven Storey Mountain*, that shows that same humanity, that same kind of confusion that makes him so utterly relatable, too. He tells about a time when he felt his friends understood

God better and were much better Christians than he. "Why was I so slow, so mixed up, still, so uncertain in my directions and so insecure?" Like Mother Teresa, here's someone so close to the heart of God yet wholly unable to see it.

20 IT CHANGED EVERYTHING

Sometime after Mother Teresa passed away, two priests were chatting about her. One said he was never a big fan of hers because he thought she was just pious, devout, and did nice, admirable works. But then when he heard about her interior life, it changed everything for him.

It changed everything for me, too. I had always had her up there on a glowing pedestal in my mind, not much lower than the angels. I had assumed that she was some other-worldly phenomenon, a one-off, mold-breaker, practically-perfect-person, sent to us by God at this very point in history to fulfill a particular mission. That's why I was so thrilled to meet her; she was no ordinary being. Or was she? "Holiness," she would insist when people called her a living saint, "is not the luxury of the few. It is a simple duty for you and for me." Mother Teresa was a human being who just kept saying yes to God every single day. The thing is, she wasn't perfect. She made mistakes because she was a human. She also became a saint.

So, maybe being a saint is not reserved just for those legendary cave dwellers of old, those medieval mystics who saw visions and heard things no one else could see and hear, or those legions of people who go about doing very good works in their white saris with the blue stripes. Maybe it's that we are *all* called to the kind of life where we too are willing to say yes to God every day, wherever we find ourselves.

21 SHE SUFFERS AND SHE LAUGHS

I n 1937, a young Mother Teresa wrote the following in a letter to her former priest back home. One of her childhood friends, Gabriela, had joined Teresa and become a Loreto Sister.

"Sister Gabriela is here. She works beautifully for Jesus—the most important thing is that she knows how to suffer and how to laugh. That is the most important—she suffers and she laughs."

This was ten years before Mother Teresa had received the call to begin the Missionaries of Charity, well before the onset of that terrible dark night. Even as a young woman, it seems, she had the insight and wisdom of someone much older and wiser.

While doing research for this book I looked for stories showing Mother Teresa's playful side and her sense of humor. There were plenty. It seemed that the more I looked, the more I found. Here are some of my favorites:

❀ In June 1993, Mother Teresa was pleased that inroads were being made for the potential of expanding their ministry into China, but apparently there was still some resistance. When speaking to the seminarians at St. Patrick's College, Maynooth in Ireland, she told them: "Especially I want you to pray for China . . . I'm giving you China, all right? If we don't succeed, I will blame you."

❀ The sisters sometimes had to make their own saris by sewing together used white flour sacks. The labeling on the sacks could not always be completely washed out and was sometimes visible through the thin cloth of the finished sari. Beneath the neat pleats across one sister's behind, the words "Not for resale" were still discernible to those who looked closely.

❀ Once, Mother Teresa was asked, "What will you do when you are not Mother General anymore?" She replied, "I am first class in cleaning toilets and drains!"

❀ Besides all the hard work and praying that made up their days, it sounds like the sisters had fun, too. They sometimes made a game of trying to beat Mother Teresa into the chapel in the mornings before 6 a.m. Mass. I read that rarely, if ever, did anyone win. . . .

- Mother delighted in the exuberant joy in the young women who came to visit in hopes of joining the Congregation. About one such group, thirty-four Missionaries of Charity aspirants, she wrote: "The Epiphany Aspirants . . . make the house vibrate with laughter."

- I once read about a situation where red tape was causing big holdups in some project and creating headaches for the folks at a Catholic organization. (I forget which one.) The gist of it was that Mother Teresa intervened and the issue was resolved in short order. Apparently, she then said to the people she had helped out, "Sometimes it helps to be Mother Teresa!"

- On another occasion, the only pair of shoes available for one of the sisters to wear to church was a pair of red stiletto heels. As Mother Teresa's biographer, Kathryn Spink, tells it: "Her hobbling appearance in such unsuitable footwear occasioned much amusement." I would not have been able to keep it together. Watching the sister in her simple white sari walk up the aisle to receive Communion in those heels would have leveled me. You can't make this stuff up.

I like knowing that being a saint doesn't have to mean living a boring life of near perfection, but can be a lighthearted, sometimes messy and fully human one. The more I get to know the saints the more I learn that they are not perfect beings. Plenty of them were far from it and would be the first to admit it. Many had terrific senses of humor and the kinds of personalities that made others want to be around them.

When I started getting to know some of the saints a few years back, I was surprised to learn that there were some whose lives I could closely relate to and would have liked to meet. St. Catherine of Genoa comes to mind. Thomas Merton is also high on my list of saints (or people who I'm cheering for, to become saints). I'd love to have known him too. The story of how he left his worldly life and came to his Catholic faith, ultimately becoming a monk and joining a Trappist order, is as surprising and compelling as any conversion story out there. I wish I could have met him and hung out with him awhile and heard him tell it. The same is true for the brilliant writer G. K. Chesterton, the mystic St. Teresa of Avila, and the Baroness Catherine Doherty, to name a few. And apparently, Saint Catherine of Siena had a startling, dark, wild kind of humor. (Sounds like my kind of girl.)

I like digging into the lives of holy people to find out what made them tick. As I dig in, some questions naturally spring up. Who made them laugh? And then I quickly think of St. Pope John XXIII, who, in reply to a reporter who asked, "How many people work in the Vatican?" reportedly said, "About half of them." Or Saint Philip Neri, who was lovingly called the patron saint of joy. And which ones had lots of friends? Who messed up and made huge mistakes, or lived lives that they would later be way too embarrassed to talk about? Augustine of Hippo, Ignatius of Loyola, and Francis of Assisi spring to mind. . . . The thing is, all of these people were striving for holiness and they all fell short. They all suffered and struggled and went through the same as us, because they *are* us.

Knowing what I do now about her interior life, I marvel at how St. Teresa of Calcutta so easily let herself goof around with Miriam and me, and that it truly seemed genuine. As Father James Martin sees it, the fact that she experienced times of doubt and anguish doesn't disqualify her from being a saint; it makes her all the more relatable. That she could also appreciate a good joke—well, that's icing on the cake.

22 TWO HEARTS

n his wonderful book *I Loved Jesus in the Night: A Secret Revealed* Father Paul Murray considers whether it's possible for two opposite conditions of soul, namely great affliction and great joy, to be present together simultaneously in someone like Teresa of Calcutta. I've often wondered the same thing about me—about any of us. Is it possible to be both? Really?

I like Bishop Robert Barron's term *vibrant paradox*. As I understand it, there are some aspects of the Catholic faith that peacefully coexist, although they might sometimes appear to be incompatible. He says it's a case of "both/and," for instance, faith and reason. Well, as it relates to Mother Teresa's experiences, I think there's something to be said for the unconventional pairing of joy and pain.

I also really like what Pope Paul VI had to say about it. He explained that the Christian believer can, in fact, "have two hearts: one natural, the other supernatural. So, very different things such as suffering and joyfulness are not only possible together, but compatible." And he says further: "The Christian can at one and the same time have two different, opposite experiences which become complementary: sorrow and joy. Thus we can say that, with her natural heart, or at the level of ordinary feeling, Mother Teresa experienced utter and complete desolation. But, at a much deeper level (at the level where supernatural grace is most at work), she was aware of being intimately united with the will of God."

Then there's the great fourteenth-century mystic St. Catherine of Siena. She writes that God revealed to her that the soul of the good Christian can, at one and the same time, be both blissful and afflicted. I was glad to discover this because it spoke to something I've tried to reconcile for years—the phenomenon that, though I might be going through the depression that visits me from time to time, I can also genuinely enjoy my children, laugh at my friend Dave's puns for the hundredth time, and delight in simple things like playing with the dog. This puzzled me. When my girls were younger, I remember watching them frolic and splash at the beach on Prince Edward Island. Those were such fun, joyful days for all of us. I also remember sitting down with a cup of tea in the evenings after the girls were tucked in for the night. I would reflect on the simple pleasures of the day. Yet I was also aware of a kind of emptiness or grief I couldn't name. I was feeling both, and it was okay. Neither of these contradictory feelings cancelled each other out. They were just there, one as much a part of me as the other. The cool thing is that I can hold both, acknowledge both, and not try to fix it or figure it all out. It just *is*. Maybe that's kind of how it was with Mother Teresa. I hope so. When I reflect on her apparent light-heartedness, it gives me hope that maybe she was able to find, among those dark and painful days, some simple joys and pleasures in the people around her, too.

23 A SAINT TO THE SKEPTICS

eople often asked Mother Teresa how she could do what she did. She would always point beyond herself, insisting that everything she had accomplished, small and powerless though she was, must be attributed to God. How else could she have done what she did? If that tiny woman from Albania could command the attention and gain the esteem of world leaders, royalty, the pope in Rome, and people of other faiths and no faith, on only the steam of her deep relationship with Jesus, all the while beset by spiritual dryness and interior pain, I wonder how much more we could do . . . I could do.

The fact that we may sometimes wonder whether God is real or question his plans for our lives does not disqualify us from the spiritual life or cause God to reject us. It doesn't mean we have nothing to contribute or that he will not answer our prayers. Consider Mother Teresa's own words on this very thing: "Yes, I have many human faults and failures. . . . But God bends down and uses us, you and me, to be his love and his compassion in the world."

Maybe, as James Martin suggests, Mother Teresa can be a model for those who doubt or are unsure about their faith. "If she could carry on for half a century without God in her head or heart," he says, "then perhaps people not quite as saintly can cope with less extreme versions of the same problem." It would seem that Mother Teresa is heading up a posthumous second ministry—only this time around it's to a "doubting world." I think of it as a kind of ministry to the poor *in spirit.* And I love the idea that now, Mother Teresa can be inspirational to a whole other subset, an entirely different crowd than the one she served during her lifetime.

Her example of perseverance despite difficulty can encourage those who struggle with their faith, which, as Father Jim has said, is probably just about everyone at one time or another. I mean, if Mother Teresa didn't have it all figured out and even, at one point, asked a priest, "Where is Jesus?"— there must be hope for the rest of us. There has to be. Clearly, her half-century struggle with God didn't prevent him from making very good use of her.

Think of it. At last count in 2015, there were 5150 sisters serving in 758 houses in 139 countries, 439 brothers serving in 77 houses in 26 countries and 35 priests serving in 9 communities in 5 countries. That's 5624 individuals, all of whom were so moved by her example that they gave their entire lives over to God's will and now carry on the work she began 70 years ago. Despite her death in 1997, the ministry continues to grow and serve the poorest of the poor on every continent. Not too shabby for a self-described worthless little follower of God! Talk about humility.

Early on in the ministry, Mother Teresa had confided in Archbishop Ferdinand Périer, telling him of the absence of the feeling that God loved her and approved of the work. When things really started to flourish and more and more missionaries were joining her, Périer told her, "You are not so much in the dark as you think. . . . You have exterior facts enough to see that God blesses your work. . . . Feelings are not required and often may be misleading." It seems she got the message and was able, in turn, to pass it on to others. One of her followers tells the story of how, when she was going through difficult times, she used to turn to Mother Teresa. "Don't give in to your feelings," Mother would say to her, "God is permitting this." The woman later said that this really helped her come through without making a bad decision by acting on her negative feelings.

"Everything she's experiencing is what average believers experience in their spiritual lives writ large," says Father Martin. "I have known scores of people who have felt abandoned by God and had doubts about God's existence. . . . Who would have thought that the one thought to be the most ardent of believers could be a saint to the skeptics?"

Mother Teresa must have had a strong sense about her ultimate supernatural ministry when she said, "If I ever become a saint—I will surely be one of 'darkness.' I will continually be absent from heaven—to light the light of those in darkness on earth." I wonder if she knew how powerful her example of perseverance would be once she had passed on and her interior life of darkness became more widely known. I do know that she told her sisters that after she passed on, she could be more help to them than she had been on earth, as she would be praying for them from her celestial vantage point (my words). I can attest to this for myself. Whenever I ask her for prayers or her help, I think I can say that she brings some light to my darkness. I've sometimes had the sense that she is encouraging me and reminding me what it's all for . . . who it's all for. That's often what comes when I turn my thoughts to St. Teresa of Calcutta: a renewed sense of purpose or a new perspective on an old problem.

I can almost hear her telling me how very much God loves me—loves each one of us. I had never really felt close to a saint in heaven before, but this is different. She's different. And because we now know what she went through in her life, it seems entirely appropriate to now christen her the "Saint to the skeptics." I wish I could see her face as she contemplates this fitting new handle. With that playful grin and a glint in her eye, I like to imagine it might make her laugh.

24 THE CALL TO HOLINESS OR, IF YOU WANT TO BE A SAINT

During his time as Pope, between 1978 and 2005, John Paul II was known for canonizing an unprecedented number of saints. One of her Missionaries of Charity once asked Mother Teresa how she could become a saint. As Father Jim Martin tells it, "The sister most likely was expecting a pious answer on living a holy life, serving the poor, and praying frequently. Instead, Mother Teresa laughed and remarked, 'If you want to be a saint, die now. The Pope is canonizing everyone!'"

As I've been thinking about what it really means to be a saint, this "call to holiness" expression I've heard around the Church for years has been puzzling me, too. I've been trying to grasp this for a while and I'm still not sure. I used to think it had to do with a flawless kind of perfection. But I think maybe it's deeper, and simpler, than that.

Father Bob Bedard, our beloved parish priest at St. Mary's in Ottawa, is a terrific example. He is now deceased, but he used to say that often his first words to God in the morning were, "Not ready Lord, but willing . . ." His remark showed a desire to please God even though he didn't really feel ready to face the day. I once heard Father Bob say that if the Lord asked him to do it, he would push a peanut down the street with his nose. He was quite the character. This reminds me of something similar Thomas Merton said. He told God that, while he believed he was following his will, he knew there was no guarantee that he was actually doing so. Nevertheless, he went on to say that he believed that his desire to please God still pleased God. I like that.

We don't have to do things perfectly all the time—or even get them right—for God to appreciate our efforts; it's more about what's in the heart. Merton once asked his friend Robert Lax what he needed to do to become a saint and was surprised by the simplicity of Lax's answer. "All that is necessary to be a saint," Lax told him, "is to want to be one. Don't you believe that God will make you what He created you to be, if you will consent to let Him do it? All you have to do is desire it." Can it really be that easy?

"Don't be afraid of holiness. It will take away none of your energy, vitality or joy. On the contrary, you will become what the Father had in mind when he created you, and you will be faithful to your deepest self," says Pope Francis.

Mother Teresa used to say that she was just a "pencil in God's hand." She made herself available to God on a regular basis and was willing to do what he wanted, plain and simple. The pencil doesn't do the work or write the words— but it lets itself be picked up and moved along by the writer.

Regardless of how she felt, this was pretty much superhuman; it had to be. The fact is that she was willing and able to get out of bed every day, sometimes on just a few hours of sleep, and do the work of providing wholehearted free service to the poorest of the poor. That a person, a human being, could do this seems to be a superhuman accomplishment. Seems this was a big part of what put her on a fast track to canonization!

By the same token, I know plenty of people who accomplish seemingly impossible, almost unbearable things, sometimes repeatedly and over many years. Parents of a chronically, critically ill child; grown children caring for a parent with dementia; spouses of military personnel who cope with their partner's absence and fear for their safety while away. . . . There are so many single parents who, despite strained financial, emotional, or personal resources somehow manage to do what they need to do, one day at a time. I know of people whose lives seem to them an exercise in frustration and, at times, utter futility. And yet, they carry on out of love, responsibility, praying for God's grace and trusting his plan even if they don't understand . . . much like their counterpart, Mother Teresa. And according to Pope Francis, the efforts of all of these good people—and indeed of each of us—are every bit as holy and heroic as anything Mother Teresa did.

As far as Pope Francis is concerned, holiness "does not require being a bishop, a priest or a religious." He continues:

"We are frequently tempted to think that holiness is only for those who can withdraw from ordinary affairs to spend much time in prayer. That is not the case. We are all called to be holy by living our lives with love and by bearing witness in everything we do, wherever we find ourselves."

When people refer to someone in a disapproving way, pointing out character flaws, or otherwise criticizing, we might hear the expression: "She's no Mother Teresa." Have you heard that . . . or said that? Well, it's a safe bet that Mother Teresa was as close to holiness as a mere mortal could be, and with good reason. Just look at everything she accomplished! And we have every reason to believe that, as Father Martin has said, people mostly assumed that "She must have been in constant close contact with Jesus, enjoying his presence, perfect peacefulness all through the years of her ministry etc." Sadly, as we know, this was not the case. But Mother Teresa was a human being who just kept saying yes to God's plan. She made mistakes. She also became a saint, but she wasn't perfect. So maybe being a saint is not reserved for the holy few. Maybe it's that simple—that we are all called to the kind of life that, though not easy or perfect, we too are willing to say yes every day and let go of the outcome. Pope Francis would agree; he reminds us that "Holiness consists in a habitual openness to the transcendent."

Mother Teresa's successor, Sister Nirmala, shared about Mother's holiness: "It was not the suffering she endured that made her a saint, but the love with which she lived her life through all the suffering. She knew that everyone can, with God's grace and one's own resoluteness, reach holiness, not in spite of the mystery of suffering that accompanies every human life, but through it."

25 HE MADE THEM LAUGH

T

hinking about St. Teresa of Calcutta and her sense of humor, it occurs to me that her divine role model must have been a lot like that, too. If we're made in God's image and likeness, it makes sense to me that he would have the best sense of humor of anyone. God, after all, came up with the concept.

I suspect there were lots more shenanigans (and maybe even pranks?) between Jesus and his apostles than a scribe could or would ever capture. I read somewhere that G. K. Chesterton liked to think that sometimes, when Jesus withdrew to be on his own, maybe he and the Father were sharing a private joke about something odd or ridiculous his beloved kids, the apostles, had said or done. (Kind of like parents who hide their laughter when their kid does something naughty but hysterical and they can't be seen taking the matter lightly.) Of course, we can't know whether there's any truth to this, but I like to imagine it.

In the movie *The Passion of the Christ*, there's a scene in which Jesus the carpenter is at home with his mother. He has been working on a table and chairs for a customer. Mary calls to him from the other room: "Yeshua!" (his name, in his native language, Aramaic). She tells him to wash up for lunch. He goes to the basin and then turns to her, splashes her and chases her with the water. She screams and laughs uproariously, trying to get away. Just then, he grabs her and kisses her on the cheek, and they're both giggling. It was such a simple, intimate moment of horseplay, over in just a few seconds. And I know it's a fictional representation of what their relationship may have been like. I know that. But there was a ring of truth. He was a man—a person. He had a mom who probably nagged him to wash his hands. We don't know for sure, but Yeshua may well have flicked water at his mother now and then. And why not? Some families are like that. If we are made in God's image and likeness, maybe we inherited some of his personality traits too, like playfulness, for example. I love the idea that Jesus may have had a wonderful sense of humor. He must have. How could we have been clever enough to come up with something like that on our own?

There's another scene in the movie where Jesus and his followers are sitting by a fire. They and many others have set up camp for the night. All around them people are busy cooking, eating, tending animals, wrangling children. And then you see it—a glimpse of Jesus whacking John with a scarf or something. Then they both erupt into laughter, and that's it. If you blink you miss it, but it was there. Again, I know it's not historically accurate. There's nothing in the Bible to suggest that Jesus and his friends had that kind of relationship. But who is to say they didn't? I mean, throughout those three years of his ministry, they traveled together on foot for days and days at a time. Walking for hours, stopping to rest, walking, stopping to find food and water, walking, then setting up camp, washing up, making simple meals, all the while spending a whole lot of time together. They spent many, many hours listening to his parables and wisdom while they walked along and sat at his holy feet listening to him as they rested. But he wouldn't be teaching them every waking moment, and do I ever wish I was a fly on the wall in those days.

What I wouldn't give to see who Jesus was when he kicked back, relaxed a little among his friends—when, very likely, he made them laugh.

AFTERWORD

Looking back on all of this now as I complete this book, I've been reflecting on those special days in India a quarter-century ago. It strikes me that if Jesus had been standing there with us in the flesh on that sad day when we had to say goodbye to Mother Teresa, he probably would have tried to lighten the moment for us, too. Mother often spoke about how she could see him in the person in front of her. In a similar way, I think that she was intentionally revealing to us something of the warmth and kindness of the Christ in her, which helps explain why people the world over were drawn to her. For me and for many, she was the next best thing to touching heaven.

Years after the trip, my six-year-old daughter Lois asked me a question that has stayed with me to this day: "Mom, who is Mother Teresa?" I talked to her about the poor people in India and how Mother Teresa and her helpers were looking after them, feeding them and praying for them. That explanation seemed to satisfy her. For a while, it had satisfied me too. But as time passed, I knew there had to be much more to it—to her. I longed to know who she *really* was. At the end of each exhausting day when Mother Teresa slipped off her sandals and placed them neatly outside the door of the chapel and entered that sacred space, who was she then? What goes on between a saint and her God?

It still makes me scratch my head sometimes, the phenomenon that was Mother Teresa. What sets apart a person like her from the rest of us? Who ends up in a place of the worst kind of desolation and singlehandedly, in just a few years, upsets the balance? It was so simple. She was walking down the street one day and came upon a man who was gravely ill. The local hospital had refused to treat him because he was poor. She bent down and picked him up. She couldn't have known that that one simple kindness would set in motion a series of events that would grow into a global ministry. Of course, she didn't know. She just saw a need and responded.

In a concrete way, she was carrying out what she later described as the "call within the call"—a kind of knowing that God was asking to leave her beloved Loreto sisters. She later said it was the hardest thing she had ever done—harder, even, than leaving her family at 18 to become a nun, knowing she would almost certainly never see them again. I have always found this part of the story terribly heartbreaking. Why, I wonder, in order to say yes to what she felt God was asking, did she have to give up so much? Why did she have to suffer like that? I can only imagine what that must have been like for her—the pain of that loss. She and her mother had been so close. But when it came down to it, they both sensed that this was to be her path. Somewhere along the way I read that she later wrote about that day. Eighteen-year-old Agnes and another girl her age sailed away on a ship toward their new life as nuns in steamy Bengal. She recalled what her dear mother had said upon her departure. It was something like this: "Look toward Jesus, take his hand and go forward. Don't look back or you will want to go back." With this new call to serve the poor, she would continue to be a religious sister, but this was to be something altogether new. God had somehow let her know that he wanted her to strike out on her own, to serve him by offering wholehearted, free service to the poorest of the poor. Before long, former students of hers followed and joined her, moved and inspired by her example, and things grew from there.

Today, as I write this afterword, it is a very cold sunny Friday in Advent in Ottawa. My two daughters, Lois and Catherine, are now teenagers. Four months ago, Catherine left for a year to pursue her own call as a Catholic missionary, serving other youth in western Canada, more than four thousand kilometers from home. In the months leading up to this as she prayed, discerned, and decided whether she would go, I often teared up, anticipating the loss I would feel if she said her yes to God and left. Eventually we both sensed that this was to be her path. As she was packing and preparing to go, I was awash with a grief I could not name, aware of an of ebbing of something I'd held onto so tightly for so long. I knew I would see her again. She would be back for a couple of weeks at Christmas, and then home for good in May. But still, this was my little girl—my first child—going away from me for the first time. The four-year-old girl who put on a brave face when her Mom and Dad split up has now grown and blossomed into a beautiful woman of God. I miss her. But she is happy and loves what she's doing and I'm so glad, so grateful to God.

Throughout this time, I've been thinking a lot about Mother Teresa and the early years of her calling. My mind keeps returning to the part of the story where she took leave of her family. Now I'm seeing it from the perspective of her mother. Again, I find this part of the story terribly heartbreaking. Why did her mother have to suffer like that—because her daughter said yes? I can only imagine what that must have been like—the pain of that loss.

I've recently read that Mother Teresa and her mother kept in contact by mail, which makes me feel a bit better about it. Apparently, Mother Teresa also wrote and sent some short articles back home to be published in the local parish newsletter. What I wouldn't give to read those articles now!

However . . . when it is all said and done . . . it is so obvious that she followed the right path. Just look at what came of it all, what God blessed and accomplished through Mother Teresa! Had young Agnes looked back, changed her mind and decided to stay home, our world today would be a very different one. It all started with a simple willingness to say yes.

ACKNOWLEDGEMENTS

I offer my heartfelt thanks to the following.

My family—Mom, Dad, Claire, Rob, Rich, Mary Ellen, Alex, Andrew, and Robbie—for their unconditional love and support, always.

Margie Lauzon, my friend, cheerleader, scribe, spiritual director, proofreader, and the loving, ever-present thorn in my side which got me to finish the book. Finally. And for all the Lauzons—our second family.

Caroline Pignat, my longtime dear friend and writing mentor for her moral support and careful attention to the manuscript throughout its numerous stages over the last twelve years.

So many cherished friends who have been my tireless cheering section all these years, many of whom have read and given feedback on pieces of the manuscript: MarieAnne Branaman, Monique De Baets, Gail Dunnigan, Jennifer Gill, Kim Hanekom, Mary Hart, Patti Hendricks, David Lauzon, Lynne McKenna, Linda Magill, Judy Masson, Sherry Milnes, Rob Parker, Pam Swords, Lisa Wood. . . . I'm sure I must be missing someone. . . . If that's you, I apologize. You know who you are.

The much-loved members of my share group, for twenty-plus years of friendship, support, some tears, and tons of laughter: Anne Marie Boswell, Celine Dumas, Collette Gallagher, Laura Kelly, Margie Lauzon, Pauline McGrath, and Julie Parker.

Dave MacLean, for his encouragement and support through the years.

Sister Rosemary O'Toole, csj, for helping me discern the India trip back in 1995 and for her caring, invaluable spiritual direction for more than twenty years.

Susan Kehoe, for her caring guidance through these many fruitful years of spiritual direction.

Dr. Daniel Doiron, for walking alongside me the past several years as I slowly nurtured the book to completion.

Rev. Susan Brandt, my friend and former employer at Ottawa Innercity Ministries, which serves those who are poor and marginalized in the capital city. Susan supported and prayed for me before, during and long after the trip. Years earlier, she wrote to Mother Teresa to ask for her advice and blessing when she sensed the call to begin OIM. Mother Teresa personally wrote back, offering her encouragement and blessing.

Jon Sweeney, my editor, for his guidance, generosity, and extraordinary patience.

Robert Edmonson for his editorial skill, kindness, and patient encouragement in the eleventh hour.

Rachel McKendree for her support and enthusiasm.

Kevin Burns, former editor of Novalis Publishing, for his interest in my book and vote of confidence back in 2007.

Lucinda Vardey, for her kind encouragement as I prepared the manuscript.

Rita Hughes, for her guidance and friendship for more than twenty years.

Ruth McGetrick, for showing the film *Something Beautiful for God* to my grade 5 class, thus, putting me on the path which led me to Mother Teresa.

Frank Lee, whose gentle spirit touches the pages of this book.

And lastly, my thanks to dear St. Teresa of Calcutta, who is indeed busily lighting the lights of those of us in darkness here on earth, just as she promised she would.

* * *

My thanks also to all the places where I've worked on this book over the years. Their hospitality is much appreciated.

In Ottawa: Al's Diner (with special thanks to Kathy . . . for keeping my coffee cup full, my spirits up, and my feet to the fire all these years); Annie's Irish Pub; Andrew Hayden Park; Arboretum Ottawa; The Art House Café; Baker Street Café; Bayshore Shopping Centre; Bridgehead; Bruyere Health Centre; Cademon's Bagel; Carlingwood Library; Chances R. Restaurant; Clock Tower Pub Westboro; Donna's Restaurant; Elgin Street Diner; The Green Door; The Green Table; Hard Stones Café; Harvey's; Heart and Crown; Ikea Café; Kettleman's Bagel; Kristy's Restaurant; Laundry Land; Moxie's Restaurant; The Newport Restaurant; Ottawa Bagelshop; Ottawa Public

Library; Reynold's Diner; Saint Mary Adoration Chapel; Saint Maurice Adoration Chapel; Saint Joseph Church; Saint Basil Church; Saint Paul University Library; Tim Horton's; The Upper Room Home of Prayer; The Wheat Berry.

In Ontario: Antrim Truck Stop Restaurant, Antrim; Heart and Soul Café, Dunrobin; Galilee Mission Centre, Arnprior; Notre Dame De La Providence Retreat Centre, Orleans; Second Cup; Starbucks; Stillpoint House of Prayer, Madawaska; The Word Guild Conference, Guelph.

In New York City: Fordham University Lincoln Center; The Watson Hotel.

My heartfelt thanks to Kelly McDonald of KMFocus in Ottawa for her expertise and generosity.

NOTES

11 *Who would have thought:* James Martin, SJ, quoted in David Van Biema's "Mother Teresa's Crisis of Faith," *Time* magazine, August 23, 2007, accessed online at https://time.com/4126238/mother-teresas-crisis-of-faith/.

78 *We are touching Christ's body in the poor:* Mother Teresa, *A Gift for God: Prayers and Meditations* (New York: HarperOne, 2003), 47.

79 *Because we cannot see Christ:* Mother Teresa, *A Gift for God*, 47.

91 *I hadn't done much:* Lucinda Vardey, *A Simple Path* (New York: Ballantine Books, 1995), 90.

110 *[T]here is in my heart:* Paul Murray, OP, *I Loved Jesus in the Night: A Secret Revealed* (Brewster, MA: Paraclete Press, 2008), 65.

111 *Interior darkness is nothing new: Come Be My Light: The Private Writings of the Saint of Calcutta,* ed. with commentary by Brian Kolodiejchuk, MC (New York: Doubleday, 2007), 22.

112 *She was a guide:* Mother Teresa, *Come Be My Light*, 312.

113n1 *She feared that her words might be a cause of scandal:* Mother Teresa, *Come Be My Light*, 379.

113n2 *If you only knew:* Mother Teresa, *Come Be My Light*, 176.

114 *Whenever I met Mother:* Mother Teresa, *Come Be My Light*, 269.

116 *to stand with us, giving us courage:* Gerald May, *The Dark Night of the Soul* (New York: HarperOne, 2005), 159.

117 *If there be God:* Murray, *I Loved Jesus in the Night*, 35.

119n1 *it was a trial of faith:* "The Light of Mother Teresa's Darkness," Catholic Online, https://www.catholic.org/featured/headline.php?ID=4792.

119n2 *This darkness was not:* May, *I Loved Jesus in the Night*, 19.

123 *with regard to those among us who feel bewildered:* May, *I Loved Jesus in the Night*, 38.

124 *Why was I so slow:* Thomas Merton, *The Seven Storey Mountain* (New York: Mariner Books, 1999), 261.

125n1 *it changed everything for him:* Zenit interview Fr. Brian Kolodiejchuk, "The Light of Mother Teresa's Darkness," Rome, September 4, 2007. https://www.catholic.org.

125n2 *Holiness . . . is not the luxury of the few:* Spink, *Mother Teresa,* xxiii.

127 *Sister Gabriela is here:* Mother Teresa, *Come Be My Light,* 24.

128n1 *Especially I want you to pray for China:* Spink, *Mother Teresa,* 271.

128n2 *the words "Not for resale":* Spink, *Mother Teresa,* 45.

128n3 *I am first class in cleaning toilets:* Murray, *I Loved Jesus in the Night,* 100.

128n4 *I read that rarely, if ever, did anyone win:* Spink, *Mother Teresa,* 47.

129n1 *The Epiphany Aspirants:* Murray, *I Loved Jesus in the Night,* 99.

129n2 *Her hobbling appearance:* Spink, *Mother Teresa,* 45.

131 *it makes her all the more relatable:* See David Van Biema's "Mother Teresa's Crisis of Faith," *Time,* August 23, 2007.

132 *Father Paul Murray considers whether it's possible:* Murray, *I Loved Jesus in the Night,* 65.

133 *The Christian can at one and the same time:* Pope Paul VI, General Audience, June 26, 1974. See "Suffering in the Christian Life," in *Pope Paul and the Spirit: Charisms and Church Renewal in the Teachings of Paul VI,* ed. Edward D. O'Connor (Notre Dame, IN: Ave Maria Press, 1978), 209.

135 *Yes, I have many human faults:* Pope Francis, Apostolic Exhortation, *Gaudete et Exsultate* (March 19, 2018), 55.

136n1 *If she could carry on for half a century:* James Martin, SJ, quoted in Van Biema's "Mother Teresa's Crisis of Faith," *Time.*

136n2 *Where is Jesus?:* Mother Teresa, *Come Be My Light,* 307.

136n3 *there were 5150 sisters:* These statistics are from The Mother Teresa Center, https://www.motherteresa.org/missionaries-of-charity.html.

137n1 *Don't give in to your feelings:* Mother Teresa, *Come Be My Light,* 337.

137n2 *Everything she's experiencing:* James Martin, SJ, in Van Biema's "Mother Teresa's Crisis of Faith," *Time.*

137n3 *If I ever become a saint:* Mother Teresa, *Come Be My Light*, 1.

139n1 *The sister most likely was expecting a pious answer:* James Martin, sj, *Between Heaven and Mirth: Why Joy, Humor, and Laughter Are at the Heart of the Spiritual Life* (New York: HarperOne: 2012), 209.

139n2 *Not ready Lord, but willing:* Rev. Robert Bedard, Founder, Companions of the Cross, a community of Catholic priests established in Ottawa. Quote from homily, circa 1993.

140n1 *he believed that his desire to please God still pleased God:* See Thomas Merton, *Thoughts in Solitude* (New York: Farrar, Straus and Giroux, 1999), 79.

140n2 *All that is necessary to be a saint:* Thomas Merton, *The Seven Storey Mountain*, 260–61.

140n3 *Don't be afraid of holiness:* Pope Francis, *Gaudete et Exsultate*, 18.

140n4 *pencil in God's hand:* From Mother Teresa's speech in Rome, March 7, 1979, cited in *Come Be My Light*, xi.

141 *We are frequently tempted to think:* Pope Francis, *Gaudete et Exsultate*, 10.

142n1 *She must have been in constant close contact*: James Martin, sj, in Van Biema's "Mother Teresa's Crisis of Faith," *Time*.

142n2 *Holiness consists in a habitual openness:* Pope Francis, *Gaudete et Exsultate*, 73.

142n3 *It was not the suffering she endured that made her a saint:* Mother Teresa, *Come Be My Light*, 337.

149 *Look toward Jesus:* Mother Teresa, *Come Be My Light*, 13.

ABOUT PARACLETE PRESS

Who We Are

As the publishing arm of the Community of Jesus, Paraclete Press presents a full expression of Christian belief and practice—from Catholic to Evangelical, from Protestant to Orthodox, reflecting the ecumenical charism of the Community and its dedication to sacred music, the fine arts, and the written word. We publish books, recordings, sheet music, and video/DVDs that nourish the vibrant life of the church and its people.

What We Are Doing

BOOKS | Paraclete Press books show the richness and depth of what it means to be Christian. While Benedictine spirituality is at the heart of who we are and all that we do, our books reflect the Christian experience across many cultures, time periods, and houses of worship.

We have many series, including *Paraclete Essentials*; *Paraclete Fiction*; *Paraclete Poetry*; *Paraclete Giants*; and for children and adults, *All God's Creatures*, books about animals and faith; and *San Damiano Books*, focusing on Franciscan spirituality. Others include *Voices from the Monastery* (men and women monastics writing about living a spiritual life today), *Active Prayer*, and new for young readers: *The Pope's Cat*. We also specialize in gift books for children on the occasions of Baptism and First Communion, as well as other important times in a child's life, and books that bring creativity and liveliness to any adult spiritual life.

The Mount Tabor Books series focuses on the arts and literature as well as liturgical worship and spirituality; it was created in conjunction with the Mount Tabor Ecumenical Centre for Art and Spirituality in Barga, Italy.

MUSIC | Paraclete Press distributes recordings of the internationally acclaimed choir *Gloriæ Dei Cantores*, the *Gloriæ Dei Cantores Schola*, and the other instrumental artists of the *Arts Empowering Life Foundation*.

Paraclete Press is the exclusive North American distributor for the Gregorian chant recordings from St. Peter's Abbey in Solesmes, France. Paraclete also carries all of the Solesmes chant publications for Mass and the Divine Office, as well as their academic research publications.

In addition, Paraclete Press Sheet Music publishes the work of today's finest composers of sacred choral music, annually reviewing over 1,000 works and releasing between 40 and 60 works for both choir and organ.

VIDEO | Our video/DVDs offer spiritual help, healing, and biblical guidance for a broad range of life issues including grief and loss, marriage, forgiveness, facing death, understanding suicide, bullying, addictions, Alzheimer's, and Christian formation.

Learn more about us at our website:
www.paracletepress.com
or phone us toll-free at 1.800.451.5006RSP)

SCAN
TO READ
MORE

YOU MAY ALSO BE INTERESTED IN . . .

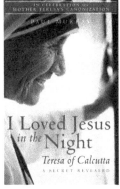
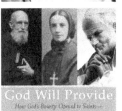
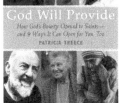